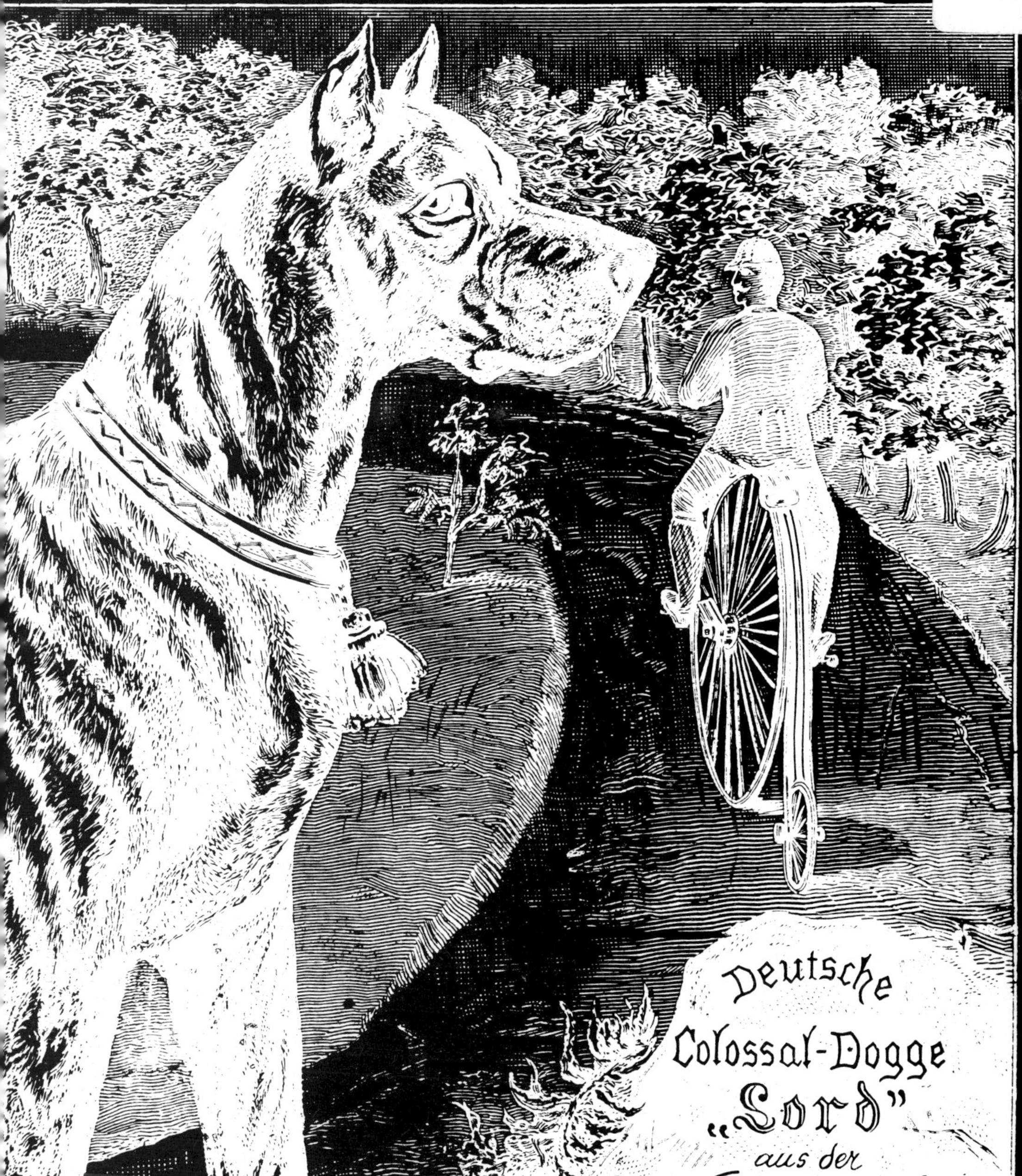
Deutsche
Colossal-Dogge
„Lord"
aus der
Race-Hunde-Zucht-Anstalt
von
Arthur Seyfarth
Köstritz

DEDICATION

This book would not have been written without the help of many friends. My sincerest thanks to all who, with their first-class photographs, helped me to illustrate the book richly.
Thanks to all the dedicated breeders for much information. Thanks for highly welcome assistance with the technical form.

DIETER FLEIG

Dr. Dieter Fleig

Translator: William Charlton

FIGHTING DOG BREEDS

IMPORTANT NOTICE

T.F.H. Publications, Inc. is the largest publisher of dog books in the world. As such we are constantly aware of popular titles in every language. Germany is famous for its excellent dog books and the leading publisher there is Kynos Verlag. They published a pair of best sellers entitled **KAMPFHUNDE I** and **KAMPFHUNDE II** written by Dr. Dieter Fleig. Dr. Fleig has an important international reputation as an authority on dogs. When we read these two books a few years ago we were concerned about Dr. Fleig's opinions about dogs and people. We were even upset about the gory details of dogs fighting dogs, dogs fighting bulls, dogs fighting rats and even dogs fighting people! Then we realized that even today there are terribly bloody fights between men, wrestling men between men and women between women. We realized that there are still war dogs, guard dogs, police dogs and hunting dogs, all of which are trained for specific dangerous tasks. But this still was not a strong enough argument for us to publish these two books and we procrastinated for two years.

Finally, after discussions with booksellers, librarians, pet shop owners and dog authorities, we were convinced to publish these two books. The argument to which we succumbed was: *Because you publish a book about wars (The Civil War, World War II, etc.) doesn't mean you advocate wars. It only means you owe history a debt to record the truth so others might benefit by the mistakes of the past.*

We have changed the names of the books from *Kampfhunde I* and *Kampfhunde II*, which literally means *Fighting Dogs I* and *Fighting Dogs II*. To more accurately describe the two volumes, our TS-270 has been titled **THE HISTORY OF FIGHTING DOGS** while TS-271 is called **FIGHTING DOG BREEDS**.

Copyright to the original German text lies with Kynos Verlag and Dr. Dieter Fleig. In 1996 an expanded version of the book was published in English. T.F.H.Publications, Inc., claims ownership of the translation and the material added to the English edition.

© 1996 by T.F.H. Publications, Inc.

Distributed in the UNITED STATES to the Pet Trade by T.F.H. Publications, Inc., One T.F.H. Plaza, Neptune City, NJ 07753; distributed in the UNITED STATES to the Bookstore and Library Trade by National Book Network, Inc. 4720 Boston Way, Lanham MD 20706; in CANADA to the Pet Trade by H & L Pet Supplies Inc., 27 Kingston Crescent, Kitchener, Ontario N2B 2T6; Rolf C. Hagen Inc., 3225 Sartelon St. Laurent-Montreal Quebec H4R 1E8; in CANADA to the Book Trade by Vanwell Publishing Ltd., 1 Northrup Crescent, St. Catharines, Ontario L2M 6P5 ; in ENGLAND by T.F.H. Publications, PO Box 15, Waterlooville PO7 6BQ; in AUSTRALIA AND THE SOUTH PACIFIC by T.F.H. (Australia), Pty. Ltd., Box 149, Brookvale 2100 N.S.W., Australia; in NEW ZEALAND by Brooklands Aquarium Ltd. 5 McGiven Drive, New Plymouth, RD1 New Zealand; in Japan by T.F.H. Publications, Japan—Jiro Tsuda, 10-12-3 Ohjidai, Sakura, Chiba 285, Japan; in SOUTH AFRICA by Lopis (Pty) Ltd., P.O. Box 39127, Booysens, 2016, Johannesburg, South Africa. Published by T.F.H. Publications, Inc.

MANUFACTURED IN THE
UNITED STATES OF AMERICA
BY T.F.H. PUBLICATIONS, INC.

T.F.H. Publications, Inc., 1 TFH Plaza, Neptune City, N.J. USA
Manufactured by TFH in Neptune City, N.J. USA

CONTENTS

FOREWORD 8

I. OLD FIGHTING BREEDS 10
   Tibetan Dog, 11; Molossus, 18; Hunting Dog, 22; The Mastiff, 26; The Bulldog, 35; Bull and Terrier, 43; The Danish Dog, 48; The Chincha Dog, 55

II. MODERN FIGHTING DOG BREEDS 59
   Tibetan Mastiff, 60; Mastiff, 65; English Bulldog, 79; Bullmastiff, 94; Bordeaux Dog, 101; French Bulldog, 107; Bull Terrier, 115; Staffordshire Terrier, 131; American Staffordshire Terrier, 135; Great Dane, 146; Boxer, 155; Mastino Napoletano, 166; Dogo Argentino, 176; Fila Brasileiro, 185; Tosa Inu, 191; Boston Terrier, 195; Herding Dogs, 198; Pug, 199; American Pit Bull Terrier, 203

III. FIGHTING DOGS IN THE FUTURE 209

FOREWORD

History of Fighting Dogs was published in 1981. It was the first book in the German language about the old fighting dog breeds. The response by dog lovers to this book has been overwhelming, and the demand for the announced sequel has become more pressing from month to month. So, today I again take pen in hand to sketch for my readers a realistic picture of the creation and development of the individual fighting dog breeds from their origin up to the present. It gives me great pleasure to write this book, for I love these beautiful dogs, with all their strength and their unique character.

A book review of *History of Fighting Dogs* by the Austrian cynologist, H. von Markusfeld, addresses the subject of man's activities in animal breeding. He comes to the following conclusion: "The question is whether man, this peculiar mammal, bred guard dogs, before turning these so-called 'working dogs' into biting machines — or bred fighting dogs, before degrading them into playthings!" In this book — unfortunately — we will continually have to concern ourselves with man, "this peculiar mammal." His doings, his breeding activities, and his whims have made unstable dogs out of many a good old breed of fighting dog. Unfortunately, man has also imitated old breeds of fighting dog and has undertaken backbreedings, the cynological value of which are justifiably very much in dispute.

What delayed the publication of the second book? Frankly speaking, I am deeply alarmed that in the twentieth century, in a civilized humanity, the incidence of mediaeval abuses is on the rise again, that today it continues to be possible to misuse dogs as fighting machines. Certainly, these people represent a tiny minority, measured

This book was originally written as part of a pair of books dealing with fighting dogs. The first book, *History of Fighting Dogs* is available as TS-270.

against the large circle of true fanciers of the beautiful fighting dogs. These "dog fighters" are first of all serious cases for the psychiatrist, and, it is to be hoped, for the public prosecutor. I found it deeply disturbing, however, that out of unscrupulous greed, personal desire for admiration, and inferiority complexes, a conscious attempt is being made to reintroduce these revolting animal fights or even to change the function of our fighting dogs by training them as "biting machines" to be used against people! And all this with the foolish argument that the unique character of these old breeds of fighting dog can be preserved in this way, indeed, that this is absolutely necessary for maintaining their good character! There are people whose relationship to the dog does not go beyond the foolish question, "Does he bite?" In this question I see the total inability of the questioner to comprehend the true inner relationship between man and dog. Dogs — particularly our fighting dogs — have a right to expect that man will not degrade them into "tools of intimidation!" "tanks of antiquity," "100-percent guard dogs for millionaires!" — how low have these people sunk who use such phrases to market their dogs. They have no idea of what an animated, affectionate, and giving creature the dog is, a friend and faithful companion in all situations. The root of the partnership between man and dog, the

FOREWORD

degree to which our four-legged friend is embedded in the fabric of the human community, lies much deeper in man and dog. My urgent advice to all breeders and fanciers if someone asks, "Does he bite?" is to throw him out the door along with his accompanying inspector. They do not have the faintest notion of the basic requirements for a true relationship between man and dog. By throwing them out the door in time, you will have saved your dog from a miserable dog's life.

My hesitation to publish this book was also based on this development. With my books I did not and do not want to open up new business opportunities for such people by making them aware of these valuable breeds of fighting dog!

I also know that some committed breeders and fanciers of fighting dog breeds could be hurt by critical comments about their breed. Critical comments are necessary, however, if I am to write an honest book. For nearly a hundred years, anatomists, veterinarians, behavioral researchers, and cynologists have stressed repeatedly that the freedom to shape a dog breed ends at the point that reckless or even intentional defective breedings are carried out. I also consider emotional and anatomical faults to be of equal importance. The breeding of large-framed dog breeds has its own serious problem: all dog breeds that are descended from the Bulldog have inherited, besides the proverbial courage and self-confidence, a wealth of anatomical faults, which are simply unacceptable in the interest of the animals' health.

Fighting Dog Breeds above all is meant to document the origin of the modern breeds of fighting dog. I do not think this is the right forum, however, for discussing current, breed-specific breeding questions, such as whether the neck should be more arched, the muzzle deeper, the bite undershot or scissors, the build rectangular or square. These questions can and should be answered only by specialists who are familiar with current breeding problems.

Naturally, this shifts the focus of my work to written and pictorial documentation. The abundance of illustrations tells its own story, of course, and shows that many breeds had already reached a state of anatomical perfection in the nineteenth century. Against this backdrop, the specialist could answer the question of whether the fighting dog breeds have, in fact, been developed further to their own and man's advantage in our time. Could this question be answered in the affirmative with all breeds?

For more than 25 years, fighting dogs have been my life's companions. I can promise this to my readers: I have written this book because I love the fighting dog breeds, because I want to communicate knowledge to all lovers of these dogs, which will make it easier for them to understand the peculiarities, strengths, and weaknesses of their own animals. If this book inspires even one breeder or fancier to work with these dog breeds to produce sound dogs of strong temperament, this would be the best justification for writing this book!

Dr. Dieter Fleig, Mürlenbach/Eifel

I. OLD FIGHTING DOG BREEDS

In my discussion of the proper classification of the breeds of fighting dog on the great family tree of the dog, and the necessity of grouping the breeds because of their great diversity, I stated previously that I am not happy with the old groupings. Fighting dogs exhibit great diversity in outward appearance. They range from the long-legged Great Dane through the heavy Mastiff, to the Bull Terrier in the terrier camp, down to the small French Bulldog and the Pug. For this reason I have emphasized seven of the breeds of fighting dog documented from the nineteenth century or earlier, which, according to my research, are the decisive foundation breeds for all current dog breeds. I am, of course, aware that these seven breeds also are related to one another. I have included the old Chincha Bulldog in my basic scheme to document the great historical age of these breeds and to prove that they developed independently of one another in various cultural circles. For many of my readers, this will be their first encounter with this long-extinct dog breed.

These dog breeds hold a key position in the development of all dog breeds. Therefore, I will discuss these breeds in considerably more detail than will be the case with the modern breeds of fighting dog. The reason for this is that quite good contemporary breed-specific material is available from numerous breed specialists.

I. OLD FIGHTING DOG BREEDS

1. THE TIBETAN DOG

The cradle of the Tibetan Dog — the oldest fighting dog breed in the world — lies in the isolation of the Tibetan highlands. This ancient religious state was once ruled by the Dalai Lama, but is under Chinese sovereignty today. It extends over an area of about one million square kilometers of high plateaus at 4000 to 5000 meters above sea level. It also has high mountains as high as the Himalayas, more than 8000 meters above sea level. The air is thin! The Tibetans, a nomadic people, over a thousand years ago bred large, heavy-boned wild dogs to protect their herds and homes from large predators. The nearly absolute isolation of the ancient religious land of Tibet and the impassability and barrenness of the Tibetan highlands ensured that the Tibetan dog breeds were bred in isolation for centuries and were not crossed with other breeds. Nonetheless, these nomadic tribes from time to time also brought a few specimens down to India when they sold their herds. These dogs interbred with the local breeds in the foothills. We find the first historical trace of the Tibetan Dog far from its homeland on a boundary marker in the kingdom of Babylon. This marker dates from about the year 1000 B.C. This stone shows a large-framed, heavy-boned dog breed with the typical tail carriage of the Tibetan. The inscription on this boundary marker speaks of Lik-Ku, the dog of the home. Strebel claims that Old Assyrian documents from this time and the translation of the inscription on the stone indicate clearly that the figure on the boundary marker represents a dog from the Tibetan highlands. We can therefore establish historically that the Tibetan Dog definitely is more than three thousand years old as a breed.

Ancient authors often mention Indian dogs, which probably were usually crossbreds of the original Tibetans and the native large dog breeds from the foothills. It is striking that all accounts unanimously indicate that these dogs are particularly ferocious and dangerous, can scarcely be controlled in their fury, and are particularly well suited for use as war dogs. In their homeland they protect the women and children from predators and two-legged scoundrels when the men leave them behind in the villages. Is it surprising, then, that modern scholars in western Tibet have proved that the dog was the highest ranking living creature after the man, and even ranked higher than the women and children (A. H. Francke)? It

Babylonian boundary marker, circa 1000 B.C.

ascended to this position as the dependable protector of herd and family. The other very important document of our Tibetan Dog is the depiction of a powerful Assyrian fighting dog. This dog is identified consistently by nearly all scholars as a typical Tibetan Dog. To substantiate this claim, scholars cite the well-developed dewlap, size (shoulder height up to 80 centimeters), strength of the animal, short ears, typical brush carriage, and extremely heavy bones. This image is on a thin tile discovered in 1854 in the rubble of the ruins of "Birs i Nimrud" in Niniveh. This temple was originally built in 1200 B.C. by a Babylonian king and restored in 580 B.C. by Nebuchadnezar. The piece of tile itself dates from approximately 640 B.C.

In the introductory discussion of the origin of dog breeds (*History of Fighting Dogs*), I stressed that I share the opinion of many scholars who believe that specific dog breeds were bred — to a great extent independently of one another —for specific purposes in many places. This means that in individual cases it is very difficult or even impossible to prove if it is a matter of native breeds or isolated specimens from other places in archaeological finds. As a rule, we have reason to believe that native dogs were depicted. Considering the value of the costly war dogs, which, of course, were usually brought to the rulers as gifts, we can reasonably assume that precisely these valuable foreign dogs were recorded for posterity by artists. The great military campaigns accompanied by war dogs are documented historically. From numerous documents we can prove that dogs from the Tibetan highlands were among the most coveted war dogs in the time before the birth of Christ.

Another problem we face in researching the Tibetan Dog is that practically no useful documents or art exist in Tibet itself, even among the nomadic tribes. The dogs found on this high plateau by individual travelers or later research expeditions, however, to a large extent agree in type and character with the illustrations documented in Persia and Assyria. We cannot prove with absolute certainty the provenance of the depicted dogs, but we can say that there is no doubt that they are dogs of the Tibetan breed type. It seems logical that these dogs could not possibly have traveled in the opposite direction. How could the poor nomadic peoples possibly have paid for expensive war dogs? Thus, scholars now agree that the Tibetan Dog, in fact, originated in the Tibetan highlands.

The Greek historian Ktesias is probably the original source for the fabulous accounts of the authors Diodor, Plutarch, and Photio. These report consistently of high mountain peaks protected and guarded by four-legged birds the size of the wolf with the feet and claws of the lion. The whole body of this animal is covered with black feathers, and the breast is red yellow in color. The vigilance and aggressiveness of this griffin prevented anyone from climbing the mountains. If we strike the word bird from the accounts of this mythical beast and replace the feathers with fur, this could be a description of the powerful Tibetan Dog, which persistently defended the high plateau and the yak herds entrusted to it against all intruders.

Aristotle (384-322 B.C.) reports of huge Indian dogs that were characterized especially by uncontrollable ferocity. Aristotle suspected that these dogs were created from a cross between the tiger and the dog, a new legend that subsequently was borrowed uncritically by many authors.

Megasthenes writes in 327 B.C. of Indian dogs with drop ears and colossal bones. They were well muscled, heavy, with huge heads and a wide muzzle. In *History of Fighting Dogs* I described Alexander the Great's encounter with Tibetan Dogs that fearlessly attacked a lion. The Greek geographer Strabon writes about Tibet in the time of the birth of Christ. Ebony was found there, and large, very brave dogs, which

I. OLD FIGHTING DOG BREEDS

Tibetan Dog, from William Youatt, London, 1850.

refused to let go when they sank their teeth in until water was poured in their nostrils. The dogs fought lions and wild steer. Some of these dogs rolled their eyes in wild rage in battle.

Strebel was the man who, besides M. Siber, has probably worked the most intensively with the historical sources of the Tibetan Dog. He explicitly distinguishes between two breeds. The first, the heavy Tibetan Dog, resembled the Assyrian fighting dogs, and certainly surpassed by far the modern Tibetan Mastiff in size and strength. The second, lighter Tibetan breed was used mainly for hunting. The heavy breed apparently was much rarer and far more coveted. Strebel writes on this subject: *The lighter form is the more natural of the two, the heavier is the one that is bred. Therefore, all heavy forms, if they are not bred carefully, always revert back to the lighter form.* Strebel sees in this a lesson for the breeding of all large dogs and is certainly right in this. The breeders of large dog breeds must fight a natural law, which dictates that the dog's anatomy, built on the wolf's skeleton, tolerates excessive size and weight only to a limited extent without incurring physical harm. Excessive size and especially weight are always to the detriment of a harmonious and functional build and the urgently necessary mobility of the dog.

From the Middle Ages, Marco Polo (1254-1323) has given us clear information on the Tibetan Dog. Marco Polo spent 25 years in the Far East, and reports from Tibet: *In this country I also found many animals that provide musk. The people of this land possess a great number of powerful and noble dogs, which do great service in catching the musk animals. The people of Tibet are a poor race; they keep dogs, as large as donkeys, which are excellent for hunting wild animals. They also keep some other breeds of hunting dogs and also have superb hunting falcons.* Particularly interesting is the reference to the hunting dogs that were used in Tibet along with the heavy Tibetan Dogs. This is clear proof for Strebel's theory, according to which various dog breeds were bred systematically for different purposes.

Between Marco Polo's accounts and the next reports from this mysterious land, about five hundred years went by. About 1800 Samuel Turner traveled to Tibet on behalf of the East India Company. Turner found the Tibetan Dog as the constant companion of the Tartar herdsman with herds of 200 to 300 yaks. The yaks grazed during the day in the surrounding mountains. At night they were herded together, penned, and guarded by several large Tibetan Dogs against four-legged and two-legged predators. Turner also found the same watchdogs in the villages and emphasizes expressly the dangerousness and aggressiveness of these dogs.

William Youatt offers an imposing illustration of the Tibeten Dog in his dog book that was published in 1850. Behind the powerful black dog tower the high peaks of Tibet. In his text Youatt relies largely on the accounts of a Mr. Bennet: *This dog is bred on the high plateau of Tibet at the foot of the Himalayan Mountains. The Bhoteas rear these dogs very carefully. When the men travel down to the lowlands, at certain times of year, to sell borax and musk, their wives and large herds remain alone at home, protected extraordinarily attentively and effectively by the big dogs. The Tibetan Dog is the dependable guardian of virtually every hut in Tibet.* On his visit to the court of the Teskoo Llama, Bennet passed a series of wooden cages, which held many large, wild, raging dogs that threatened him. They were native Tibetan Dogs and either were so ferocious by nature or infuriated by their confinement. They were so aggressive that Mr. Bennet did not dare to approach even slightly closer to the cage. Anyone who reports on these dogs speaks of their unusual size, their proud appearance, their ferocity, their pronounced aggressiveness toward all strangers. The dogs are described as being of a deep-black color, somewhat lighter on the flanks; only the legs and small spots above the eyes are of a red or light-brown color. As with the Mastiff, the muzzle is very broad, short, and deep, but the flews droop even more than in the Mastiff. The coat hangs quite loosely all over the body.

Strebel, based on all the accounts available to him about the Tibetan Dog in its native environment, portrays it in a photogravure, in the middle of the Tibetan highlands as a guardian of yaks.

It is no wonder that, considering all the impressive and charming accounts

Tibetan Dog, from Richard Strebel (photogravure), 1905.

I. OLD FIGHTING DOG BREEDS

Tibetan Mastiff, *Siring*, from Hugh Dalziel, London, 1881.

of this legendary dog breed, the first importations to England and the Continent attracted great attention. The first Tibetan Dog was donated in the late 1860s by the future King George IV to the new Zoological Gardens in London. In 1876 another pair arrived from India. Dalziel depicted the male of this pair in 1881 in his book.

Further importations followed, but always sporadically, because it proved to be extraordinarily difficult to get to Tibet through India and — once there — to acquire a truly good animal of this breed. The long sea voyage and the great difficulty of keeping the dogs healthy while acclimating them from the high-altitude climate of Tibet to Europe made importation extraordinarily more difficult.

Among the successful importers before the turn of the century was a Mr. Brooke, who provides us with the following account: *A principal trait of this breed is its body size, the larger, the better. The dog's front must be particularly good, with particularly heavy and strong, straight front legs. In comparison, the hind legs are surprisingly weakly developed. This, along with the wolf claw, is a further parallel to other dog breeds from the mountains. The lionlike mane stands erect from the full coat; its ruff strengthens the impression of imposing size. In its homeland this dog is used to guard the herds and the huts, which is its main function, and as a pack animal to carry heavy sacks of salt. It is best suited, however, to defend against predators. For this purpose it is often equipped with a spiked, iron collar, which naturally detracts greatly from its typical ruff. Its outer coat is very dense and stands out from the body. It also has a heavy undercoat. As a rule, its color is black with tan markings, sometimes also pure black; occasionally, red specimens also occur. Its luxuriant tail is usually carried high, often curled over the back.*

Its head type lies between the Bloodhound and the Mastiff. It has powerful jaws, which it needs both to fight the leopard or wolf as well as to hold down a wild yak.

The top of the head is rounded, the skull and face are covered with folds of skin. Its eyes are small and deeply set, and part of the conjunctiva of the eye is visible.

At the borders and in the outlying regions the size and type of this dog breed quickly fall off the pronounced traits of the breed degenerate through crossbreeding, and we are left with only a normal-looking animal the type of a normal sheepdog.

The true type of the mountain dog is an unmistakable, true mastiff. The black of its coat is velvety and completely different from, say, the black of a Newfoundland.

In 1904 Major Dougall brought the male dog Bothean back from an expedition to Tibet. He too complains that the old, powerful type of the true Tibetan Dog is becoming increasingly rare. He writes the following about Bhotean: *His character is that of a pronounced 'one-man dog.' I could do anything with him, but he retained an insurmountable aversion to all strange men; however, he never tried to attack a woman or child. On walks he had to be kept on a leash; I could not let him run free. In the beginning I kidded myself into thinking that I had acclimated him properly, and so let him run free — with catastrophic results! It proved impossible to cure him of the fault of immediately regarding all strange men as personal enemies. He was a superb watchdog, always wide awake at night, resting during the day . . . Tibetan Dogs are quite sociable and faithful to their master but are quick to take revenge for punishment and hold grudges for a long time. If we scold them occasionally, show strictness, then, despite kindness, they become submissive slaves. Naturally, we can do nothing to change the true nature of this dog, and part of this nature is to view each stranger as his master's personal enemy. They take no notice of strange dogs, as long as they do not bother them. They are indifferent toward women and children, and every child is under the best of care with them.*

These Tibetan Dogs were brought to Europe at the beginning of the century as precious objects and were the sensation at many dog shows.

Tibetan Mastiff, *Bhotean*, London, 1912.

I. OLD FIGHTING DOG BREEDS

Tibetan Mastiff, *Aylva*, engraving from Bylandt, 1897.

Because of their ferocity, the private buyers often gave them to zoos, where attempts were also made to breed them. The long journey and the extreme climatic changes rarely agreed with the dogs. In their homeland the type declined sharply after the turn of the century because of inbreeding.

Allow me to make a final comment. There is the suspicion that the numerous old accounts of the sizes and weights would scarcely stand up to rigorous examination. The requirement for maximum shoulder height is always cited as evidence of the great size of these dogs, but none of the imported dogs that were measured were larger than our sheep dogs with respect to shoulder height. Mr. Brooke's D'samu, for example, had a shoulder height of 61 centimeters and weighed about 45 kilograms. At the turn of the century, Strebel made detailed measurements of four Tibetan Dogs in Germany. The male dog had a shoulder height of 65 centimeters, one of the three bitches measured 62 centimeters, and the other two were 59 centimeters at the shoulder. Unfortunately, Strebel did not provide information on the dogs' weights, but they could not have exceeded 50 kilograms. Were these dogs already evidence of the decline of the breed?

We conclude by considering the imposing Tibetan Mastiff on the Continent. An engraving from the superb dog book by Count Bylandt from the year 1897 shows the bitch Aylva. This illustration underscores once more the strength and imposing stature of the Tibetan Dog and also shows the relatively low-slung build of the dog.

2. MOLOSSUS

Is it a shame if I openly admit that after quite diligent study of various authors their idea of the Molossus seems very vague to me? On the one hand, most cynologists today believe that a molossoid dog is a member of the old fighting dog breeds. On the other hand, they make seemingly logical deductions about the type of fur, ear position, and functions to show that historically documented Molossus is the ancestor of a number of herding dogs. On this subject, however, I share the opinion of Rittmeister von Stephanitz, who rightly stresses that local breeds of guard dogs were bred for the task at hand from local dog breeds. The idea that simple shepherds brought expensive fighting dogs from foreign lands to improve their dogs does not seem likely. It seems more sensible that these valuable fighting dogs were imported to improve the local breeds as war dogs.

Let us now turn to the facts. Ancient Molossis, from which these dogs certainly take their name, is a part of Epirus and is located on the

Molossus statue of the Nikias in the Vatican.

northern west coast of Greece. Today Epirus is part of southern Albania. Ancient Epirus was the center of power of the Molossis, a Greek tribe that had intermarried with the original Celtic inhabitants. In Molossis there was an oracle to the god Jupiter, the Holy Oak of Dodona, that was visited by many religious pilgrims. The pilgrims sought advice from the oracle. These pilgrims are said to have developed a lively export trade in aggressive, large-framed dogs from Epirus. The pilgrims brought these dogs to their homelands, where they continued to breed them or used them to improve native breeds.

The Frenchman Mégnin and a number of other scholars believe that the Molossus was nothing more than the descendent of the Tibetan Dogs that Alexander the Great brought to Greece, which had found a new home in Molossis. Other scholars, including Strebel, consider the Molossus to be an independently bred, large, native dog of this land.

I. OLD FIGHTING DOG BREEDS

Aristotle (384-322 B.C.) praises the Molossus: *In Molossis there is a breed of dog, which serves as guardian of the herds, which distinguishes itself from all other dogs through its size and indomitable courage against wild animals!* The author Marius Terentius Varro, who died in the year 27 B.C., reports in his book on agriculture of two kinds of dogs that were bred in this country. The first were hunting dogs and the second large herding dogs, who effectively protect sheep and goats. From his description of these herding dogs we quote: *The lower jaw is undershot. From it grows two teeth, one on the left, the other on the right, which are only slightly exposed . . . These dogs have large heads and drooping ears, a strong nape and neck . . . The tail is thick, the bark sonorous, the jaws large; the color usually is white, so that it can be distinguished from predators at night.* We often find reports that native dog breeds were substantially improved in form and character by crossing them with the Molossus.

The dispute between the scholars concentrates on the question of whether the Molossus was usually white in color, which would support the thesis that they were mainly herding dogs. Because of their white color, the shepherds would be able to see them more easily at night, and distinguish them more readily from predators. Other finds document that the Molossus was black in color, like the Tibetan Dog. These accounts mention large-framed guard dogs, whose dark color served as camouflage.

Another controversial point is the ear type. Drop ears, as described by Varro, should prove descent from the Tibetan Dog, prick ears would be considered proof of the independent development of the breed, even for the crossing in of wolf's blood. Scholars use the famous Molossus statue of the Nikias in the Vatican as proof for their theory. With this statue, however, I cannot help thinking that we are looking at a cropped ear. This theory has other inconsistencies as well, such as the fact that heavy, large dog breeds usually have heavy ears.

The finds in the palace of the Assyrian King Assurbanipal (668-636 B.C.) in Niniveh are considered to show the very typical Molossus. A small terra-cotta depicts a large-framed Molossus with a splendid drop ear. No one could imagine the Assyrian war dogs in the mural from the same palace with prick ears, or could they? Again, typical Molossus!

Strebel is correct in demanding that we seek out evidence in the nearly unintelligible jumble of ancient sources. In the following discussion of the history of the origin of the Mastiff, and later the Bulldog, we will learn that originally clearly fixed concepts over time become vague generic concepts. Naturally, this hinders any study of the sources.

It is documented that in Molossis itself, large, aggressive dogs were

Molossus terra-cotta from Niniveh, circa 650 B.C.

Mural from the palace of Niniveh, circa 650 B.C.

systematically bred, that these dogs were used principally to guard the herds, but that they were also superbly suited for use as war dogs. Apparently, in peacetime the white dogs stayed with the large herds and the black ones guarded the human settlements. Whether they were drop ear, prick ear, or cropped ear, we could certainly argue this point at length. Who can guarantee, though, that the figures of dogs with prick ears actually portray the Molossus? The size and weight of the dog certainly would very much favor a drop ear.

There is no controversy that these Molossus largely had an identical anatomy (we were also able to demonstrate this with the Tibetan Dog). When we come to the modern breeds of fighting dog, we will find that several of them still serve as large herding dogs. Fighting dogs and herding dogs are capable of defending themselves; we found the same situation with the Tibetan Dog!

Let us read what Professor Studer writes on this subject in his book *Die Rassen des Hundes* in 1894: *Whether this portrayal . . . gives a clear picture of the dog, and whether in antiquity the name Molossus came to be used for large dogs in general, these questions I will leave aside and instead call attention to the following facts: In the region of Molossis in Epirus, large dogs were bred as watchdogs, which were called Molossus from their provenance. The region was in the vicinity of modern Lake Janina.*

The Molossus belong to the tribe of the

I. OLD FIGHTING DOG BREEDS

Illyrians, who invaded northern Greece from the north around 1200 B.C., drove out the Hellenes, and occupied Epirus in their place. The descendants of the Illyrian Epirians are the modern Albanians.

The rugged mountains of Epirus, which, outside of the fertile valleys, doubtlessly only permitted cattle breeding, especially sheep breeding. The herds were guarded by large dogs. They were prized for their strength and vigilance, and were soon exported to Greece and Italy as watchdogs.

A large number of antique statuettes, mosaics, and murals depict such watchdogs; the most beautiful image of one is the famous statue of Nikias in the Vatican. Such portrayals are distributed through Greece, Italy, and southern France. All show the same breed, a muscular dog with prick ears, occasionally drop ears as well, a sharp head with an elongated, more or less broad snout, and a heavy, manelike coat on the neck and nape, which in some extends to the front legs . . .

It would probably not be far from the truth to say that the term Molossus changed over the centuries from the name of the original geographic provenance of the dogs into a generic name for large, aggressive dogs throughout the Continent.

To conclude on the Molossus, let us refer to our illustration of Conrad Gessner's guard and fighting dog (*Canis bellicosus et homines defensor*). It is a true Molossus. Gessner writes in 1669 about this dog: *There are certain dogs that are bred to protect man and to fight, and which strike like murderers. These are said to be large, gaunt and loathsome but also strong and bold, and they were also equipped to fight armed men. They are said to recognize no other man and to love only their master. They do not allow any other to touch them and obey and protect their master alone. They are trained and equipped with skill for battle.*

Alexander Pheraeus, a great tyrant in Thessaly, is said to have bred an exceedingly large and horrible dog, which was every man's enemy, except for those that fed him. He kept this dog as a doorkeeper or guardian of his bedroom,

Canis bellicosus from Gessner.

because he did not feel safe from the people who opposed his tyranny.

The King of the Garamants, when he was in exile, returned from exile to his kingdom with two hundred dogs, because they had fought so well against his enemies.

The Gessner animal book further describes the duties of our Molossus: *There is another kind of dog that protects farms and ships. Those that are used to guard and protect farms are said to be altogether terrible in voice and appearance, have a terrible head, be completely black color, and have a short body. Not with their voice alone, but with their frightening appearance as well, they could chase away thieves and rogues. Also of the same form are said to be those that are kept to protect the helm of the ship and the merchant's goods.*

There are also some dogs that are kept by common people to protect the house from thieves or other unsavory people. They were commonly used by the ancients and are still used by many in our times.

3. HUNTING DOG

It is recorded in history that the Germans always brought large, ferocious dogs on their military campaigns. Roman historians reported of powerful dogs that defended bitterly the German laagers and the women and children.

Bull Biter, Bear Biter, and Boar Hound are various names for one and the same fighting dog. The collective term *Hunting Dog* — for male dogs as well as bitches — comprises all the large, native German hunting breeds.

We know how this Hunting Dog was used to hunt dangerous game and refer particularly to the many illustrations of these hunts. The Hunting Dog was usually kept in large packs at the courts, in accordance with the feudal system of the day. The medieval hunting system demanded a breed like the Hunting Dog for hunting the aurochs, bear, and boar. Considering how dangerous these opponents were, the old Bull Biters always paid a high price in blood — boar's heads cost dog's heads! So, the original war dog was turned into the essential, brave Hunting Dog.

In Germanic law from the fifth and seventh centuries A.D., these Hunting Dogs were recorded in writing for the first time. The law even distinguished between Bear Catchers *(Canis ursoritius)*, Boar Dogs *(Canis porcaritius)*, and Bull Biters *(Canis qui vacaam et taurum prendit)*. In chapter 83 of the Germanic law, anyone who intentionally kills such a valuable dog must pay a large fine: *If someone kills a good Boar Dog, which seizes the boar, a Bear Dog, which seizes the bear, or a Bull Biter, which pulls down the cow or bull, he must pay a fine of three solidi.*

Strebel is correct in saying that at this early time it is out of the question that imported English Mastiffs had already been crossed in; rather, the Hunting Dog was a separate dog breed bred in Germanic lands, descendants of the large war dogs that had defended the Germanic laagers.

It is interesting how scholars repeatedly search for proof that specific dog breeds were purebred Indian dogs, Molossus, or Germanic Hunting Dogs. In doing so they do not properly take into account the enormous distances between the individual centers of breeding. Certainly there were human migrations, military campaigns, and some contact with traders. Certainly a few dogs went along on some of these journeys, and they may have occasionally mated with the local breeds. Considering the large number of good dogs people needed in those days to hunt and to protect the farms, such outcrosses could not have played the slightest role in shaping these breeds. This did not change until later, when dog breeding with breeds deliberately imported from foreign lands was pursued at royal courts.

Dog reliefs dating from the twelfth century are preserved in the cloisters of the great cathedral in Zurich. They depict the large Germanic Hunting Dog hunting boar and bears. As we have seen, the Tibetan Dog and the Molossus were large herding dogs, ferocious dogs, which were used mainly to protect herds of livestock. In the Germanic realm the large hunter, the Hunting Dog, dominated. This certainly tells us something

I. OLD FIGHTING DOG BREEDS

about the difference between the dog keepers! The herdsmen and farmers had their Tibetan Dog and Molossus, the courts of the nobility had their Germanic Hunting Dog.

The first importation of English Mastiffs is mentioned in 1406 by Gessner. Johann Täntzer in 1699 gives a detailed account of these English dogs. He tells of their usefulness in the hunt, and how they were bred with the old Hunting Dog to improve the bite very hard. *The forehead is broad between the eyes. These dogs are stout and heavy, their gait is strong and ponderous, but they are uncommonly fervent in the chase, and attack so stubbornly and fiercely that they tremble with rage and are hard to pull away from their victim.*

Flemming distinguishes one dog as the *Dantzicker Bear Biter*, which he considers to be a dog from the underworld or other ferocious type of

Danzig Bear Biter, from Flemming.

breed. In his account, Täntzer distinguishes very clearly between the English dogs, crossbreds, and the unchanged old bull biters.

Hans Friedrich von Flemming, in his book *Der vollkommene teutsche Jäger*, which was published in 1719, gives us a vivid picture of the Bear or Bull Biter: . . . *of medium size, but rather thickset, with a broad chest, a short and broad head, short, upturned nose, stiffly erect, sharply cropped ears, very strong jaws, which allows them to* dog. *Then they are very mean, unfriendly, and fierce and are superior to other dogs. They are used particularly on Polish or Hungarian bison hunts, as well as sometimes to hunt bears, and they prove to be most useful on such hunts.*

Flemming then speaks further of a somewhat lower dog, in all other features, however, similar in build, the Brabant or Dutch Bull Biter. As the name implies, it was bred not to hunt, but to bite bulls. Both dog breeds had cropped ears and docked tails. He

emphasizes that they had extraordinarily strong bites and that they often sank their teeth into their opponent.
Otherwise, these dogs, because they are of a bad disposition, are sturdy of body, and have a very loud bark, they are most useful as good guard and tiedogs. They are always very alert and ferocious. These dogs are usually short of nose and black around the mouth. The lower jaw is undershot. They are yellowish or brindled in brown and their eyes are very unfriendly and bad tempered.

It must be emphasized that Flemming bases his descriptions on his own observations, which — unfortunately — is not true of all chroniclers. Many an account — we of course documented this with the Tibetan Dog — is based on hearsay. Thus, the Brabant Bull Biter was used primarily for bull baiting, in the same way as in England, whereas the larger Danziger Bear Biter was a ferocious hunting dog used to hunt bear.

Johann Elias Riedinger (1698-1767), the famous engraver from Augsburg, who was almost a contemporary of Flemming, also portrays bear hunting with the Bear Biter. Riedinger is rightly

Danzig bear biter, from Riedinger.

considered a great expert in all questions on hunting, and his entire body of artistic work is characterized by the painstakingly precise reproduction of all details. We are indebted to this artist for two splendid illustrations of these dogs. His Brabant Bull Biter is a large, yellow dog with a dark mask. It has a particularly pronounced head and stands on sturdy legs. His Danzig Bear Biter has a slightly longer coat, is probably brindled, and is a large, powerful, heavily boned dog.

To illustrate this, observe the folio by the Frenchman Charpentier, with anatomical studies of the Bull Biter in that country. The clear similarity to Riedinger's engravings is astonishing. The massive dog's head shown with the drop ears demonstrates that not all these dogs had their ears cropped.

In Winckell's *Handbook for Hunters and Those Entitled to Hunt*, we find at the beginning of the nineteenth century a clear endorsement of the old Hunting Dog. Admittedly Winckell recommended it only for hunting bears, not for hunting the wild boar, because it was often injured seriously because it refused to let go of the boar. Concerning the bear hunt,

Brabant Bull Biter, from Riedinger.

I. OLD FIGHTING DOG BREEDS

Winckell says: *The Bull or Bear Biter is a not too large, but strong, brave dog breed with a broad, short head. They grip everything that they are set on, but they are heavy. Their ears are cropped and their tail is docked before they are six weeks old. Because of their fierceness and meanness, they can easily become dangerous to people and animals; for this reason, in several countries it is not permitted to make use of them.*

From J. M. Bechstein we can infer the rampant occurrence of cleft nostrils in the Bull Biters. These double nostrils were not considered a fault at the time, but rather as a very good quality. The uglier, the more frightening the better! This philosophy is very difficult for the average dog fancier to understand, but it is very widespread among the supporters of the old fighting dog breeds. In this book we have to come to terms with this phenomenon many more times. For the moment we wish only to present it as a fact, as a fact that for the sake of the grotesque, breeders even bred for serious pathological symptoms. Bechstein describes the "Bull Biters with the harelip," which he gave the Latin name *Canis fam. lagochilus: the upper lip is either completely split, so that the teeth are visible, or only to the base, so that there appears to be two noses.*

In the *Monographie des Hundes* by Th. Gotz from 1834 we find a rather good description of the Bull Biter: *The head is uncommonly broad with a deeply inward curving nose, which is usually split in the middle of the nasal bone. Hence, such dogs also go by the name 'double nose.' It is extraordinarily powerful and has a ferocious, mean temperament, but is willing to sacrifice its body and life to protect its master and his possessions.*

This dog breed is used frequently in Vienna to hunt animals, a popular barbaric pastime in Viennese society, where a single dog often must fight a bear or an auroch. The best ones are found on farms, where they often fetch very high prices.

They do excellent service on journeys and are kept by jailers to guard the prisoners. The famous robber chief, the so-called Hundesattler, kept these dogs, from which he got his name.

Its color is usually fawn yellow with dark, dirty brown markings and stripes; there are brown ones as well; in all, however, the front part of the head to behind the flews is black.

To return for the moment to the subject of the double nose, Professor Hilzhimer states in his book about the Chincha Bulldog that the double nose in the old Bull Biter was considered a virtually infallible indication of purity of the breed. Unscrupulous dog traders gave the impression to the gullible buyers that the keenness and aggressiveness of the breed was inseparably coupled with this split nose.

Dr. Fitzinger, in his notorious book *Canis Molossus Palmatus*, which was published 1876, construed from this that the double-nosed Bull Biter represents the pure, unadulterated breed. Besides the completely split nose, Fitzinger states that another infallible character of the breed is the *strongly developed membranes between the toes* of the hind feet, thus a kind of webbed foot. For this reason he claims that this dog is the best swimmer of all dogs! Fitzinger's description also includes the interesting observation that this dog constantly drools in long strings from the flews.

We can establish that, in the course of centuries of development, two dog

I. OLD FIGHTING DOG BREEDS

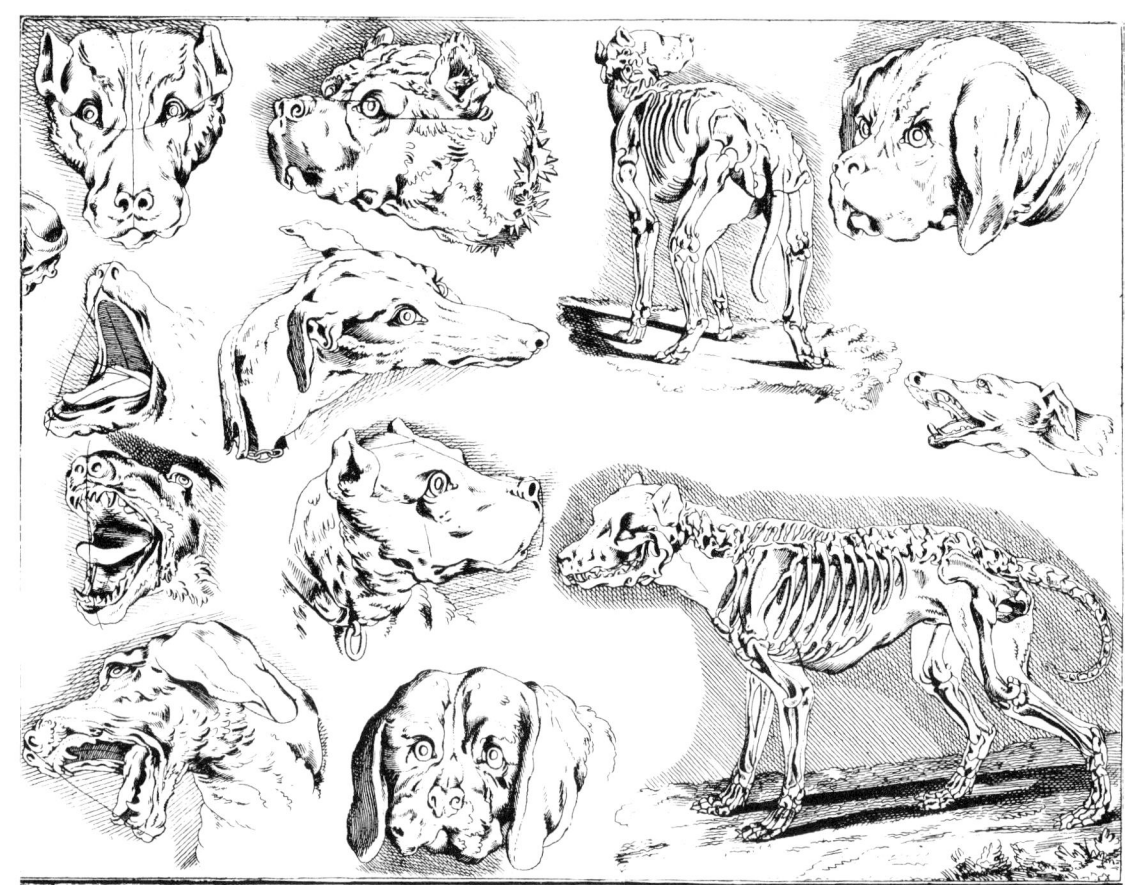
Studies of the Bull Biter, by Charpentier.

breeds formed from the large, old Hunting Dog. One was a large, long-legged, somewhat more agile dog — the ancestor of the modern Great Dane. The other was the stocky, broad-headed, heavy Bull or Bear Biter, probably along with the English Bulldog the foundation breed of the modern Boxer. Goschel reports that the last old Boar Dogs documented in Germany were bred at the hunting court at Kassel in the Electorate of Hesse. The last true Boar Dogs were sold in the year 1876, after which breeding ceased. Since then this dog breed — unfortunately — must be considered as extinct, although it continues to live on in the Boxer.

4. THE MASTIFF

The English Mastiff is justifiably considered to be one of the most magnificent dog breeds in the world. Naturally, with the Mastiff we again immediately face the question, did this dog breed develop independently, in Britain alone, or were the Tibetan Dog and Molossus its ancestors? The advocates of the theory that this is a purely English breed base their argument on the account of the Roman author Gratius Falsius from the year 8 A.D. He writes of big exhibition fights in the amphitheater of ancient Rome between the pugnaces from Epirus — that is, the Molossus — and the pugnaces from Britain — that is, the early English Mastiff. In these exhibition fights it turned out that these wide-mouthed dogs from Britain were far superior to the Greek Molossus. Their

I. OLD FIGHTING DOG BREEDS

victories in these exhibition fights established the reputation of the English dog breeders. Falsius reports: *Although the British dogs are distinguished neither by color nor good anatomy, I could not find any particular faults with them. When grim work must be done, when special pluck is needed, when Mars summons us to battle most extreme, then the powerful Molossus will please you less and the Athamanen dog cannot measure up to the skill of the British dogs either.*

Strabo, another Roman, reports in the year 38 A.D. of large English dogs, which were bred in their homeland of Britain to hunt dangerous game and as war dogs. When they conquered Britain, the Romans encountered these dangerous dogs, who together with their British masters offered the Romans stubborn resistance. The courage of these dogs was so impressive that the Romans shipped them back to Rome as war booty for the exhibition fights in Rome. A Roman officer, the *procurator cynegii*, was stationed in Winchester and was responsible for selecting these dogs and shipping them to Rome.

Thus, the Mastiff is, in fact, an ancient English dog breed, for during the conquest of Britain these dogs already proved to be superior in combat to the Molossus the Romans brought with them!

There are a number of prominent scholars who do not, however, rule out the influence of the Tibetan Dog and the Molossus on the Mastiff even at this early time. It is certain that as early as 600 B.C. Phoenician traders came to the Scilly Islands and Cornwall to trade Greek goods for coveted English metal. It is certainly possible that these traders also sold large Molossus to the inhabitants of the region. The Molossus would have improved the small, but extraordinarily courageous, native dogs, and a connection to the Tibetan Dog and Molossus would have been established.

A rather pointless argument! As a matter of fact, there are few sensible reasons why the inhabitants in each region could not have developed the desired dog breed for specific purposes. We need only consider the enormous range of variation within the dog species, from the toy to the colossal Great Dane! Accordingly, it is of absolutely no importance whether the Mastiff received a few shots of Molossus blood as a result of this early trading. The Mastiff is certainly an ancient English dog breed!

Linguists have also tried to make inferences about the provenance of the dogs from the meaning of the word *Mastiff*. In his book *Zur altesten Geschichte des Hundes,* Dr. Albrecht uses comparative linguistics to study the origin of the names of dog breeds. Citing the similarity of the names used in various regions for large dogs — *Mastiff, Maytin,* and *Matîn* — he concludes that these European dog breeds must have had a common root. He considers the common root of these terms to be the Latin word *Mausuetus* meaning domesticated. Other linguists trace the origin back to the Latin word *Massatinus* meaning domestic. The accuracy of this linguistic analysis is not in question, nor are the etymologies, which refer to the traits of these large dogs. It seems completely mistaken to me, however, to infer the relationship between these dog breeds from this. Far more logical is the observation that Latin had an influence on virtually all European languages, and that dogs with similar purposes accordingly were given similar names from the same Latin root.

Permit me to make one final linguistic remark. The Old English name for the

Mastiff is *mase-theve*. From this we can derive the term *master of the thieves*. A completely different etymology in the Germanic language leads to the Low German *Mast-teve*, a term for a heavy, stocky dog.

A jump of several centuries carries us from the combat arena of ancient Rome to the immense forests of England in the fifteenth century. In the oldest English book on hunting, *The Master of the Game*, we can read about two large English dog breeds, the Alaunt and the Mastiff. The Duke of York describes the Alaunt as a large, powerful dog. Its purpose was to hunt wild boar as a boar hound; however, it also assisted the herdsman and butcher as a brave herding dog. We will return to this Alaunt in our discussion of the English Bulldog. On the subject of the Mastiff, the Duke of York writes in 1406 in *The Master of the Game*: *It is the job of the Mastiff, in keeping with its nature, to protect the animals, house, and farm of its master. It is a good breed of dog, for it protects and defends with all its might all its master's possessions. It must be of an unfriendly nature and of decidedly frightening appearance.* The Duke adds that there are also some good Mastiffs that also help professional hunters to bag good meat. The Mastiff — like the Alaunt — could also be used to hunt wild boar. The main purpose of the Mastiff, however, in contrast to the Alaunt, was to protect its master's possessions.

From Dr. Caius, physician in ordinary to Queen Elizabeth I, we learn from the year 1550: *The Mastiff or 'ban-dog' is a coarse, very large dog with a broad, heavy head, ugly and quite keen, of heavy, ponderous form, and thus not too fast. It is horrible and frightening to see how much more ferocious and aggressive it is than any Arkadian Dog (Molossus). It is said of it that it is descended from the lion. This dog is also called 'Villatica,' because its job is to guard and protect farms . . . It is a dog of ferocious courage and aggressiveness. Its look fills the heart of men with fear. These dogs fear nothing in the world, no weapon forces their retreat or disheartens them.* Dr. Caius reports further that the Mastiff is often systematically trained as a war dog to attack people, and he praises its fearlessness in attacking the bear, bull, or wild boar. During training the human opponent is equipped with spear, club, or sword, but these duels only serve to make this dog become stronger and more self-confident.

We are indebted to Aldrovandus from the year 1637 for a very vivid description of the Mastiff in the Middle Ages: *When this dog attacks huge bulls and bears, it tries to grip them and hang on. It continues every fight, even if badly wounded. Its ears hang low, its flews fall loosely, it is ferocious in appearance and has a strong neck. Its head looks flat from the side, blunt when viewed from the front. The Mastiff has large, rounded paws with soft pads, the knee has a strong joint, the body is not too heavy. The legs must be completely straight, the loin long. The backbone is solid, the loin robust. The color is red brown, the chest fits well with the rest of the body. The dog gives the impression that it breathes fire from its nose, its voice fills the forests with an intimidating baying and releases the anger from deep in its breast. At the same time its eyes glow, its nape swells, and often it curves its tail in a ring over its hairy back.* We are also indebted to Aldrovandus for a good woodcut, which he calls the *English fighting dog of frightening appearance*. We could quote a number of other witnesses to the noble appearance of this dog. These descriptions are so similar, however, that there can be no doubt that the old English Mastiff was one of

I. OLD FIGHTING DOG BREEDS

the most splendid and valuable dogs in England during the Middle Ages.

In *History of Fighting Dogs*, we presented what is probably the earliest oil painting of the Mastiff, by Abraham Hondius from the year 1635. The strength, the anatomical build, and the aggressiveness of these two dogs fighting the dangerous boar are impressive. A number of other hunting pictures from England in *History of Fighting Dogs* show the Mastiff hunting dangerous game.

The breeding of the Mastiff was in the hands of large, reputable families, mostly from the high nobility. The Lyme Hall Mastiffs had an almost legendary reputation. This kennel was located in Cheshire. Its animals were of unusual size and strength, but had a considerably longer muzzle than was subsequently desired. The history of this kennel goes back to October 25, 1415, the day of the battle of Agincourt. The British won a significant victory here over the Gauls. Peers Legh of Lyme Hall fought on the victor's side, but was found by his comrades badly wounded on the battlefield, his faithful Mastiff bitch at his side. She refused to leave her master's side as he was carried away, not even on the long road to Paris. She followed her master's coffin when he went to his final resting place in Lyme Hall. The Legh family founded their Lyme Hall line with this faithful bitch; the direct descendants of the bitch were never sold. In a clear instance of close family breeding, the Legh's built up the Lyme Hall Mastiff.

English fighting dog of frightening appearance, woodcut from Aldrovandus, 1637.

A total of four large old kennels stand out. We have already discussed the Lyme Hall line. Next in importance is the Chatsworth line of the Duke of Devonshire. The third significant kennel was built up by Lord Harrington under the name Elvaston Castles, and the fourth line, Hadzor Hall, belonged to the old Gatton family. Mastiffs from these four English top kennels made the dog famous and celebrated throughout England.

It is alarming to read as early as 1803 in the *Sportsman's Cabinet*, that the good old Mastiff was becoming more and more of a rarity. Crosses with various other dog breeds had caused a serious decline in the quality of this large breed. A true Mastiff had now truly become a treasure. This old breed differed from the crossbreds through its special substance, shoulder height, bones, and strength. Attention had to be paid to heavy ears, strong flews, and the spirit of the dog. The majesty of the appearance of this dog combined power and strength. The dog stands on the southern bank of the Thames in front of some old warehouses. On the opposite bank, St. Paul's Cathedral is clearly visible. The dog depicted here agrees to an amazing degree with the quoted accounts. It has the broad forehead, medium-length muzzle, heavy ears, strong flews, powerful but stately,

I. OLD FIGHTING DOG BREEDS

Mastiff, from D. Reinagle, 1803.

arched neck, long but firm back, heavy bones, first-class paws, and quite attractively angulated pasterns and hocks. Take special notice of the good, powerful body without any sign of overloading of the dog.

Now another interesting observation by the author of this book, who was a "veteran sportsman," is that the aggressiveness or good nature of the Mastiff is largely determined by how it is kept by man. If its living space is restricted, it becomes very aggressive. Chaining it leads to extreme ferocity, even viciousness. If the Mastiff is given plenty of room to move about on a large property, this dog tends to be good-natured and attacks only when truly endangered. This description of the temperament is confirmed by many other accounts.

Professor Gmelin, for example, writes of the Mastiff in 1792 in *The Animal Kingdom: The Mastiff fulfilled its mission as a watchdog with great loyalty, even with intelligence. Some allow a stranger to come onto the guarded property and then walk peacefully alongside the intruder across the property, as long as he does not touch anything. But the moment the stranger touches an object or dares to leave the property again, the Mastiff makes*

I. OLD FIGHTING DOG BREEDS

everything clear. First it warns with a quiet growling, and, if this does not help, it makes it clear by its rough manner that the stranger may neither do harm nor walk away. This dog does not use force as long as you do not offer resistance. He who does not acquiesce is seized, knocked down, and held in the same spot, if necessary for hours, without the dog biting seriously. This continues until the owner frees the intruder. This is truly a watchdog that many a dog lover dreams of.

We are indebted to the painter, W. R. Smith, for a very attractive picture of the Mastiff, which we have taken from the famous book by Jesse from the year 1846. Here we see the Mastiff as an imposing watchdog in the countryside. This large watchdog is protecting the property, and with a very good anatomical build despite its great size!

Allow me the pleasure of presenting another superb portrayal of the Mastiff. The animal artist Denay created a Mastiff bronze in around 1850, which shows how perfectly the size of the dog, heaviness of the bones, head type, and first-class anatomical build can combine with one another. I consider this to be a true challenge to any Mastiff breeder to breed again such a fundamentally sound, beautiful dog, which still has the old Mastiff character.

Rawdon R. Lee writes in 1899 of the unmistakable decline of this beautiful old dog breed. He says that breeders

Mastiff, from W. R. Smith, 1846.

Mastiff bronze, by Denay, circa 1850.

have perpetrated gross exaggerations in striving to achieve extreme head forms, and that breeding in general is becoming a burden to the proper symmetry of the breed. He criticizes sunken backs, bowed leg bones, and atypical, rolling gait. He claims the dog is getting further and further from its former position as the king of dog breeds.

Leighton looked back in 1912 with sadness to the old days, when — as he reports — in about 1871 in the Crystal Palace in London, 63 Mastiffs were still shown: *Not a bad dog among them!* After the turn of the century, he saw a real decline in the dog breed. He says that with this breed in particular breeders are no longer aware that utmost care is necessary in breeding as well as keeping. The Mastiff must always be kept in proper condition. When the dog is confined to cramped kennels, as is generally the case, there is the danger that it will become too heavy. He criticizes especially the increasingly weaker hindquarters.

Drury writes in 1903 that the breed is losing more and more fanciers, that it is bred too much for a head with an extremely short muzzle, while overlooking completely all other important characters. He complains of too short bodies, short legs, poor angulation of the hindquarters, straight hocks, loss of substance, and faulty gait.

These rather randomly selected accounts about the Mastiff from the beginning of the twentieth century document that massive faults were already appearing in the breed at that time, which continue to plague the breed today. I have carefully studied the

I. OLD FIGHTING DOG BREEDS

literature from the turn of the century and have been unable to find a single author who did not criticize the decline in quality of this dog breed! This is surely food for thought! Can it actually be the case that this large dog really needs a much larger living space for proper development? Consider the wide living spaces in the countryside, where this dog fulfilled its duty as a watchdog, consider the great hunts, the huge kennels in the old castles! Does this dog breed — and many other large breeds along with it — suffer from the lack of space, which they were not developed for?

Let us put this question aside for the moment and return to the development of the Mastiff at the end of the nineteenth century.

The Old English Mastiff Club, England was founded in 1872. Its purpose was to further develop this dog breed and to support the breeders and fanciers of the breed to the best of its ability. I have shown in commentaries dating from thirty years after the founding that this goal obviously was not met, that faulty development was perhaps even encouraged by mistaken breeding goals.

First, however, let us take a look at the dogs that stood at the top in England at this time. Many experts of the breed believe that the breed was in its heyday during these years.

The male dog Turk was considered to be one of the best Mastiffs in England and was the sire of many good dogs. The dog was whelped in 1867 and traced its ancestry back to the famous Lyme Hall line. The enormous sum of 500 pounds was paid for it in 1868. A comparison of Turk and the Mastiff by Reinagle depicted in the *Sportsman's Cabinet* at the beginning of the nineteenth century documents clearly the improvement of the breed within the nineteenth century.

One of the most beautiful Mastiff pictures of all time shows the male dog Wolsey, who was whelped in 1873. Wolsey also traces its descent back to the old Lyme Hall line. When he compares this dog to the bronze by Demay, many a fancier will raise the objection that Wolsey carries too much weight. At one time, however, the ultimate goal of breeding was majestic size!

Mastiff *Turk*, seven years old, 1874.

We know that Wolsey weighed 61 kilograms and had a shoulder height of 77 centimeters and a chest circumference of 104 centimeters. I am impressed with the picture of this dog because it puts the Mastiff in an appropriate environment, as the dog of the large, old country estates and castles.

Let us close this section with a word from the Mastiff expert, Sidney Turner. He was the leading founding member of the Old English Mastiff Club. Turner writes in his splendid *Encyclopedia from the Year 1910* of an obsession among Mastiff breeders with their one-sided breeding for a short muzzle. On the subject of the true type of the Mastiff, he stresses: *There is no more noble-looking dog, surely few nobler looking animals at*

Mastiff *Wolsey*, 1876.

all, than a well-proportioned, active Mastiff! On the other hand, there is scarcely a more pitiful sight than a crippled giant! What would become of our impression of the most attractive of people if he had a crippled back and stumbled over his own legs? What do you think of a noble thoroughbred with a dream head, if it no longer has a single healthy leg to stand on? Why in the world should the head of a dog be the excuse for all the other faults of its anatomy? Turner writes emphatically that the overemphasis of breeding for heads has degenerated the Mastiff into a monstrosity!

Maybe it is only proper with this closing observation to leave the Mastiff in its state of development just after the turn of the century. Certainly it will be a good place to start up again with the discussion of the modern Mastiff.

5. THE BULLDOG

We cannot overestimate the importance of this dog breed for all dog breeding. Up to the present day, the entire English people are identified with this dog breed. The

I. OLD FIGHTING DOG BREEDS

Bulldog became the symbol of the English nation (John Bull). There is no other breed of dog that elicits such divergent feelings. The scale of feelings ranges from extreme loathing to unbridled admiration — indeed, almost reverence. In this connection, the feelings are not limited by any means to the judgment of the character of the dog, but rather also extend to its outward appearance.

The historical background of the Bulldog shines blood red. This breed of dog was bred to fight mercilessly, even to the death. We have reported in detail on this subject in *History of Fighting Dogs*. The illustrations shown there speak for themselves.

In *The Master of the Game* by the Duke of York, we find in 1406 a historically unambiguous source that describes clearly the character and anatomy of the Alaunt. Of importance in this book is the clear distinction of the Mastiff and Alaunt as separate breeds. Only two of the three breeds of the Alaunt described in the book could be the ancestors of the Bulldog: the Boar Hound of the hunter and the Bull Biter of the butcher. The "friendly Alaunt" described in the same place, with great hunting ability, is more likely the ancestor of the Irish Wolfhound and Deerhound.

Alaunt Ventreres and Alaunt of the Butcheries are the two breeds that interest us. We read: *The Alaunt is of better outward form and stronger than any other animal, when it is a question of attacking another animal . . . No matter how you look at it, Alaunts are completely unpredictable, take offense at everything. They are crazier and more rabid than any other hunting dog.* The Duke of York describes the Alaunt as being similar to the Greyhound in outward appearance, except that it has a very large and broad head with heavy flews and ears. It is used primarily for bull biting and for hunting wild boar. Characteristic of the breed is that it always sinks its teeth into its opponent and then can scarcely be forced to open its jaws again. As a rule, Alaunts are heavy and very ugly dogs. For this reason it is no great loss when they are killed by the bull or boar. The Alaunt is also used by butchers in the town to drive cattle. A single dog can hold an escaping ox. The Alaunt is used for bull baiting and prove themselves particularly useful for flushing boars when other dogs do not dare to enter the thicket.

This description of the Alaunt shows that it clearly was a large, heavy dog with a prominent skull, an aggressive and self-confident dog, which certainly could be dangerous. It was considerably larger than the future Bulldog, since it, of course, was also used on the hunt. Its other functions, however, already resemble closely the reason why the Bulldog was later systematically bred.

The first source in which the word Bulldog appears is a letter from the year 1630. In it two good Bulldogs were ordered in London from St. Sebastian, Spain. They were to be sent as soon as possible by ship. The Spanish demand reads: *They must be good with bulls and can cost whatever they may as long as they are truly good.* This provides clear proof that good English Bulldogs were exported early on to Spain, the land of bullfights.

We do not wish to go into the numerous individual portrayals of the Bulldog from the seventeenth to the nineteenth centuries. They could fill a separate book. They prove, however, how controversial this dog breed already was at that time. From descriptions it is evident that in anatomy and character the Bulldog was bred for a single purpose: bull baiting. A long-legged, fairly large dog was still needed for running the bull. For bull baiting, which almost always was practiced with a bull tied on a rope, the fighting technique required for this task determined the anatomy of the dog.

The Bulldog had to get down as low as possible and work its way toward the bull with its belly dragging on the ground. This technique exposed the least surface to the opponent's horns. Then, depending on the bull's carriage, the dog would make a mighty leap at the bull's mouth. Now it needed powerful jaws, as strong as a vice, to get a firm grip. Play low, pin and hold! Creep up on the belly, bite, hold on mercilessly: these were the tasks for which the Bulldog was bred over many, many dog generations.

Hugh Dalziel, in his book *British Dogs* from 1889, worked out surprisingly well how anatomy and character make up a solid whole in this breed. He emphasizes the specific traits and the consequences of the anatomical build as follows: *Short nose, large and massive head with broad muzzle. The broad muzzle is the most important of all and is the fundamental requirement for its task* (sine qua non). *The larger the circumference of the head, as a result of the heavy cheek musculature, the more muscle power presses the jaws together. The shorter the muzzle, the stronger the grip. The broader and flatter the muzzle is in front, the broader and larger is the bite. The lower jaw is undershot, which enables the dog to grip the bull's nose from the front, and allows it, once it has gained a grip, to hold on tight. The lobes of the nose slope back, so that air can stream freely into the nose, even when the dog has a firm hold. Obviously, if the lower jaw did not extend in front of the nose, the nose and jaw would be on the same plane, and the nose would be pressed completely flat against the part of the body into which the dog has sunk its teeth. This would be extremely detrimental to breathing. In such a case the dog would not be a true Bulldog, equal to all its tasks.*

The Bulldog's body is like that of a proper man: broad and deep chest, well muscled between the shoulders, narrow in the waist. Because of the deepness of the chest and the strong, muscular shoulders, the front legs appear short. Its back is short and powerful; long-backed dogs are weak, slow, ponderous, tire easily and have a loose, swaying, and uncontrolled gait. The hind legs are strong and muscular, and produce an abundance of power to drive the body forward. They are similar in length — proportionately — to those of the Greyhound. Accordingly, the loins arch upward, higher than the shoulder. Because of this the dog can launch itself suddenly into the air. The body must be proportionately small, the belly tucked up under the loins. The flanks are hollow, to save as much useless weight as possible.

Is it not fantastic what thoughts were already held about the correct anatomy of a dog at this early time? Dalziel's explanation reads as if an engineer had been given an assignment to build the most effective fighting machine against the bull! Some things that appear senseless, even grotesque today, at one time absolutely made sense for the function of a Bulldog.

With pleasure I use this opportunity to present several of these old Bulldogs. The famous *Wasp, Child & Billy* from 1809 was by the famous animal painter H. B. Chalon. Of great interest is the original inscription of this print: *The Bulldogs portrayed above are the property of Henry Boynton and are descended from*

I. OLD FIGHTING DOG BREEDS

the kennel of the Duke of Hamilton. They are the only ones that remain from this line and are valued so highly that Mr. B. declined an offer of 120 guineas for Billy as well as the offer of 20 guineas for a pup that had just been whelped by the bitch. It was assured that these are the only Bulldogs from this line and that after their death this dog breed must be considered as extinct.

This is a splendid portrait of these last representatives of the line of the Duke of Hamilton. It is interesting that even in the year 1893 these dogs were still considered to be ideal examples of good Bulldogs. The brindle sitting dog was considered to be the best of the three.

It is fortunate that the breed did not actually die out with the death of these three dogs, so we can turn next to the famous print "Crib and Rosa" taken from a painting by A. Cooper from the year 1817. This print made Bulldog history. Rosa was the Bulldog that breeders held up as the breeding goal in the nineteenth century. The bitch was even expressly featured as the breeding goal in the first standard of the breed by the English Bulldog Club in 1875. Crib was Rosa's son. Take note of Rosa's elegance, of the first-class anatomical build with straight, strong legs and superb angulation. I could imagine that even today many a dog fancier would still gladly call such a beautiful and good dog his own.

A few years later we come upon "Lucy," a print made in 1834 from a painting by Smith. Lucy was a rather famous Bulldog bitch. In her, as well, we can study the power and good anatomical build of the breed. In 1830 the English animal painter, J. T. Tuite, painted a white contemporary of this bitch. This is a rather heavy male dog, fairly long in the back, but with a rather good, prominent head.

The breed suffered a very serious setback when all animal fights were legally banned in 1835. Many feared that the breed would die out. From the old fights the breed had acquired a quite dubious reputation among all dog fanciers. We have also described previously the circles of the population that kept these dogs at the beginning of the nineteenth century. The dog suddenly became virtually worthless to them, because it no longer brought in the big money. One of the last holdovers from the old days was the London dog dealer, Ben White. He owned his own pit, and his Bulldog kennel had a first-class reputation up to his death in 1838.

Wasp, Child & Billy, hand-colored print from H. B. Chalon, 1809 (Dr. Flieg's collection).

I. OLD FIGHTING DOG BREEDS

Crib and Rosa, hand-colored print from A. Copper, 1817 (Dr. Fleig's collection).

Lucy, hand-colored print from Smith, 1834 (Dr. Fleig's collection).

I. OLD FIGHTING DOG BREEDS

Male Bulldog, oil painting by J. T. Tuite, 1830 (Dr. Fleig's collection).

We show this pioneer of the breed in a very rare print, of which only six copies were ever made. Taken from a painting by J. C. Scanlan, we present: "Ben White, running his Bulldog 'Tumbler'" and "Lady Sandwich's Bess against Bill Gibbon's Bull." If we did not have the clear caption, many a Boxer fancier would see in these dogs the Boxer of the 1930s. These dogs also demonstrate the anatomical soundness and mobility of the Bulldog in the nineteenth century. The diminution of Gibbon's bull lay within the scope of the usual artistic freedom of the painter.

It is the unanimous opinion of all authors that in the difficult years after the fights were banned, England's lowest classes prevented the British national dog from dying out. These efforts led to their appearance at the first dog shows. The breed was cultivated particularly in the center of London, Birmingham, and Sheffield. The first best in show for a Bulldog was won in 1860 by James Hinks from Birmingham. It is interesting that this was the same James Hinks who created the Bull Terrier at about the same time.

The first standard of the breed was

Bill White, Tumbler & Bess, engraving, circa 1860 (Dr. Fleig's collection).

written in 1865 for the Bulldog. Its author was the Bulldog man, Samuel Wickens. This standard entered into the history of the breed as the Philo Kuon standard. Noteworthy is the foreword to this standard, with the general description of the breed: *The British Bulldog (Canis pugnax) is a very old, majestic breed of dog. It has become very rare, has been much mistreated, and as a rule is very poorly understood. If we treat this dog with kindness, give it much attention, and if it lives together with its master, it is a calm, pleasant dog. If it is kept as a yard dog, if the company of its master is lacking, it becomes less sociable and gentle. If you bait it, however, and make it vicious, then it becomes one of the most dangerous of animals. In general, it is an excellent watchdog, an extraordinarily good water dog, and is particularly valuable as a breeding partner for terriers, pointers, hunting dogs, greyhounds, and so forth. It supplies courage, determination, and stamina to these dog breeds.*

It is the most fearless and strong-willed animal. The fighting cock is certainly a very courageous bird, but it will only attack another of its own kind. But there is nothing in the world that a good Bulldog will not attack at any time, always all out and with exemplary courage. It will not give up until it is dead.

This noble dog degenerates in foreign lands — it truly is an animal of the nation, completely identical with Old England — it is a dog that every Englishman can be proud of.

Worth noting is the statement that the Bulldog was crossed into many other dog breeds, primarily to improve their substance and courage. Lord Orford, for example, crossed Bulldog blood into his Greyhounds at the end of the eighteenth century over six or seven generations and determined that he could retain the proverbial courage of the Bulldog in his dogs. Crossing the Bulldog with the Terrier produced the splendid Bull Terrier and the Staffordshire Bull Terrier. We must also realize, however, that highly undesirable anatomical faults were also brought into all these breeds.

It was justifiably said against the criticism of the character of the Bulldog that the majority of the critics had never owned a Bulldog themselves, and that they accepted uncritically the exaggerated horror stories and questionable reputation of the breed, which had been damaged by the role it had played in the *cruel sports*. We must also understand that the Bulldog's temperament arose over many dog generations from its use as a fighting dog breed. The pit was a cruel master. Only the dogs that survived the merciless selection process here, both physically and emotionally, lived to breed.

I again quote here from Hugh Dalziel, quite simply because I believe that his words have a significance that goes far

I. OLD FIGHTING DOG BREEDS

beyond the history of the Bulldog: *In the 'good old days,' when this dog was still at home in all levels of society, its spiritual abilities were valued so highly that the Bulldog was declared the symbol of the national character, its famous 'Bulldog courage' and its determination were praised. These traits — carried over to the people — turned England into a world power.* Dalziel claims that the Bulldog was rejected by the upper classes after the fights were banned. It continued to survive in the lowest classes of society, where it was used in illegal dog fights. This led many authors to confuse the true character of the dog with that of the people who misused this dog for their own purposes.

Ch. Bulling Passion — Bouledoguisme, 1901, from R. H. Moore.

Give a dog a bad reputation, and hang him!' This is an old catchword, which unfortunately has also been applied to the Bulldog. *'The virtues of this dog are its own. The burdens and viciousness are those of its master!'* The Bulldog is in fact simply a dog — no more and no less — and he can, like any dog, be his master's friend and companion.

As with children, the dog's spiritual abilities are developed through upbringing and experience. It is true that 'The God of the dog is man!' When, therefore, a dog is treated by man as if it were the devil incarnate, when it is trained using the roughest methods and misused for the cruelest and most dangerous purposes, then its master will destroy all its good traits.

When its master takes pride in the ferocity of his dog, should we be surprised when this animal, which survives all the cruelty that has made it vicious, is then purported to have a vicious character by those who fear it? When love and affection are wrongly suppressed, when an animal is chained and kept alone to increase its ferocious tendencies, this animal learns to view man as its enemy. The dog is prepared to return the brutality that it receives daily. Any breed of dog kept and treated in this way will become vicious, assuming that it has enough courage to survive all these trials.

If the Bulldog, however, is kept and nurtured with the same love and care given to other breeds of dog, then there is no other dog in the world that adjusts so well to all its master's demands and can serve him as well as this breed!

Permit me to elaborate upon Dalziel's words by stating that all breeds of dog descended from the old Bulldog place more demands on their owner than do other dogs. An expert on this problem rightly claims that these dogs tolerate no fool as their master.

Moreover, there are two sorts of fools! The one — the more dangerous —

awakens the ferocity slumbering in this breed, turns it into a real danger to himself, his family, and the people around him. The other, more harmless fool, accepts too little responsibility and has too little insight to turn the dog into a respectable citizen through proper training. In each case we must say that any complications that arise are not the dog's fault, but its master's.

The Bulldog Club of England, which was founded in 1875, succeeded in saving the breed from extinction and turning the old fighting dog into a show dog. Whether this dog breed has fared well in the long run will be the subject of further discussion. To begin with, the Philo-Kuon Standard was adopted in full with only a few minor corrections.

It is rare but, as with the Mastiff, breeding for the show ring does not seem to have helped the Bulldog. Breeders are very prone to viewing individual breeding goals in isolation and then exaggerating them.

Drury writes in the year 1903 that the Bulldog, at the turn of the century, was a totally different animal than the Bulldog from the middle of the nineteenth century. The active, long-legged fighting Bulldog was transformed into a very low-slung, heavy, compact dog. He describes it as a calmer and friendlier dog. It is very difficult to enrage, but then reacts with the fury and persistence of its ancestors.

An alarming warning sign of the aggravating changes in the outward form of the dog was the modification of the standard by the Bulldog Club. The Bulldog expert, Edgar Farmann, writes on this subject, in his monograph on the Bulldog, that in 1894 the Bulldog Club had no choice but to delete the old reference to Rosa from the Bulldog standard. By that time the breed had already moved so far from this ideal that it was ridiculous to claim that the Bulldog was bred toward this ideal. We see, then, that this modification of the standard was not a timely advance at all, but the end of a sound breeding direction.

Farmann reports further that at the end of the nineteenth century, as a result of intensive inbreeding, the vitality, mobility, and fertility of the Bulldog had declined sharply.

On this subject, I must make a very serious comment. The famous French scholar, Pierre Megnin, in his book *Le Chien*, discusses a genetic disease, which he calls bouledoguism. This is a degenerative disease, which affects particularly the head area of the dog, but also the trunk and legs, and which appears frequently in the Bulldog and its relatives. Megnin illustrates this development with the picture of the Bulldog Champion Bulling Passion taken from England in the year 1901. This bouledoguism was seen as a form of rachitis.

Bouledoguism is characterized by the following symptoms, which are usually linked:

a) the shortening of the upper mandible that breeders strive for, but to such a degree that the undershot bite is exaggerated, readily recognized by the "flashing" fangs;

b) the extreme shoulder development occasionally also observed in Basset Hounds. There is no connection to the shoulder, except that the front legs support the dog's body from below like columns, and the thorax hangs loosely from the ligaments of the shoulder area;

c) the legs are, as a rule, distinctly shortened and thickened. Megnin reports that, as a result of this disease, individual specimens of the large breeds degenerate into pronounced dwarf forms. Instead of fighting against this

I. OLD FIGHTING DOG BREEDS

dangerous disease, in England a separate show class was created for these kinds of degenerate dwarf forms, which have even been show winners. Megnin reports from his own experience that dogs afflicted with this genetic disease look nearly normal as puppies. The first signs of the disease become apparent when the puppies from the mother show pronounced deformities in the second dentition. The full extent of the deformities is apparent only in the fully grown dog.

We have here an early indication that abnormalities are bred for in the Bulldog and the breeds of dog influenced by it. Scientists in our century have criticized widely the increase in abnormal breedings. We should take these observations as a warning not to overlook the fundamental goal of breeding sound dogs at the expense of breeding for exaggerated characters. This applies particularly to all dwarf forms of dog breeds.

"Playing Bulldogs," by the artist L. Jennings from 1914 shows the power, substance, and anatomy of the Bulldog. It is an impressive work of art and is considered to be one of the best works on the Bulldog.

6. BULL AND TERRIER

Is it not surprising that we present here a cross between two dog breeds as a separate old fighting dog breed, even though its name indicates that it is a cross and not a dog breed with its own standard?

Playing Bulldogs, bronze by L. Jennings, 1914 (Dr. Fleig's collection).

Nonetheless, the Bull and Terrier holds a key position in the history of the breeds of fighting dog. The crossing of the two old English dog breeds produced dogs that were perfectly suited for the repulsive, but highly fascinating, dog fights. We have presented at length to what extent the dog fight had an almost magical fascination for the broadest social strata in England. The old prints and numerous accounts offer clear proof of the kinds of dogs that were used to fight in the pit.

Analagously to the history of the origin of the Bulldog, the anatomy and character of the Bull and Terrier were the result of selective breeding for a single purpose: to fight. In the case of the Bull and Terrier, this meant the fight of dog versus dog. The opponent of the old Bulldog was the bull. The decree "Go low, pin and hold!" led to anatomical changes in the originally long-legged, mobile dog: a lower-slung dog with bent front legs, loose shoulders, roach back, strongly undershot bite, and an iron grip on whatever it pressed between its jaws.

Such a dog was unsuitable for fighting other dogs in the pit. Once the dogs went at each other and got a good grip, there would be little left for the spectators to see, except for two dog bodies gripping one another, each dog closing its jaws tighter and tighter, gripping mercilessly. Missing here, however, were the quick attacks, ever new grips and tricks, which made up the drama of a dog fight that appealed to the base instincts of the spectators, gamblers, and dog owners. The Bulldog fought according to its talents: pin and hold. This largely excluded the breed from the big business of dog fighting.

What could be more obvious than to cross terrier blood into the Bulldog? Longer legs, fiery temperament, speed — thus providing attractive fights, which was the goal. In the early nineteenth century, the terrier breeds were first-class working dogs, keen rat and vermin dogs, sparkling in temperament, quick to bite. Stonehenge writes that in those years in no other country in the world were such good vermin destroyers bred as in England. He stresses in his book, *The Dog,* published in 1859, that the keenness of the English terrier breeds was usually achieved with a shot of "Bulldog blood." This was the only way to explain the exceptional insensitivity of these dogs to rat bites. Other dog breeds fearfully avoid rats, whereas the terrier itself does not give up even when a half dozen rats hang by their teeth from its loins. Here we have more clear testimony of the degree to which the English Bulldog improved the substance of dog breeds, which most dog fanciers are totally unaware of.

Ash writes in his book on the history of the dog: *The crossing of the early form of the Bulldog with terrier breeds had the result that a lot of dogs and bitches were produced that no longer belonged to the foundation breeds. As a result they became quite attractive in appearance, their work was substantially more successful, and gradually a new breed of dog arose. These were bred exclusively for the dog fight, for rat biting, for drawing the badger, in general, for attacking animals of all sizes.* These claims are substantiated by the good illustrations of the fighting scenes pictured in *History of Fighting Dogs.* Ash also claims that the famous fight between the lion and the dogs in Warwick from the year 1825 involved dogs of the Bull and Terrier breed. In the meantime we have found another illustration of this fight, a print from the year 1825 by W. Menath.

Trusty, Lord Camelford's Bull and Terrier, Sporting Magazine, 1806.

It is downright striking how closely the lion dogs of Warwick resemble the famous dog Trusty. According to accounts in *Sporting Magazine* from the year 1804, Trusty, on account of his wonderful fights, was just as famous throughout England as the Emperor Napoleon. This dog changed hands from one famous dog fighter to another for large sums of money. He first belonged to Humphrey, then Johnson, then Ward, who sold him for the handsome price of 20 guineas to a Mr. Mellish. Lord Camelford was so deeply impressed by the fights of this male Bull and Terrier that he bought Trusty from Mr. Mellish. In accordance with the tradition of the country, the sale was "on the carcass way," that is, the weight of the animal was paid for in gold at a price of two guineas per pound weight of the dog. Trusty weighed 42 pounds and therefore brought 84

I. OLD FIGHTING DOG BREEDS

guineas for his owner. It would have been an insult to the noble animal, however, had this sum been paid in money. Accordingly, Lord Camelford handed over his favorite gun valued at 40 guineas and a pair of particularly beautiful pistols valued at 44 guineas and became the proud owner of Trusty. Finally, the Lord gave the dog as a present to the famous English boxing champion, Jem Belcher. The Lord stated that only an undefeated man was worthy of calling this unbeatable dog his own. Trusty had gone undefeated in 104 dog fights. "In our time no other dog in all England can prove descent from better fighting dogs or more noble blood!" This was the opinion of all the fans of this crossbred Bull and Terrier in 1804.

In his outward appearance, Trusty showed very clearly its descent from the Bulldog. The dog Dustman, whose picture we have from the *Sporting Magazine* from the year 1812, exhibits a distinctly stronger terrier infusion, a substantial improvement in its anatomy. The magazine described Dustman as a very famous and talented fighting dog, which represented the optimal type to strive for. The breeding of these dogs was becoming increasingly more important, and the Bull Terrier enjoyed the highest esteem throughout England.

Another illustration, "Rattle and Clinker, the Halfbred Dog and Terrier Bitch", is an attractive hand-colored print. It was taken from a painting by S. Alken and was published in 1822. Rattle is the large half-Bulldog, half-terrier dog. Note its truly appealing anatomy, a pied coloration, long leg bones, very good angulation, elegant head, which definitely calls to mind the modern Staffordshire Bull Terrier. We can assume that this dog had a normal bite, not an undershot bite. In *Sporting Magazine* of 1822 we read that the new dog breed to a great extent had now found its own constant form.

Dustman, Bull and Terrier, Sporting Magazine, 1912.

An oil painting by an unknown painter dates from a somewhat later time, about 1830. It shows the Bull and Terrier of the Viscount Purst. This dog is particularly interesting because its skull seemingly would even meet the strict requirements of the modern judge. The combination of self-confidence, strength, and good anatomical build are impressively documented in this painting.

Stonehenge writes of the newly created breed of dog: *In reality, for all tasks that the terrier is used for, the half or quarter crossbred, which goes by the name Bull-Terrier, is much more valuable than any of its purebred ancestors. If such a dog is to be truly useful, however, it must be more than half terrier, otherwise it will be too awkward or too slow, have too much of an undershot bite to be able to grip well with the fangs, and show too little obedience to dependably obey its master's commands. When bred in this way, the Bull and Terrier is the fighting dog par excellence, and in actuality there is scarcely a task that you could use a dog of this size for that it could not do just as well, usually far better, than other dogs. In ferocious aggressiveness, combined with obedience and a good nature, paired with intelligence, it exceeds any breed of dog in existence today.* To breed the correct type, Stonehenge recommends three or four crosses, with the foundation breeds and the first products of the cross. This will produce the ideal Bull and Terrier.

Finally, let us consider Sting, from *Stonehenge's Book of the Year 1859*. It is descended from the Nottingham line, one of the best lines of fighting dog. It is interesting that Stonehenge describes it as a Bull-Terrier despite the dark color. He stresses that the new dog breed is considerably stronger than the original terrier breeds. Breeding with the Bulldog had given them much more courage, stamina, and resoluteness. The terrier, in turn, had lent symmetry and a harmonious build to the new breed.

Pierce Egan, one of the best portrayers of the sporting events in the first half of the nineteenth century, sketches the following portrait of the newly bred dog breed: *This new breed is without doubt highly suitable as a life's companion for active, venturesome young men, whether they travel on horseback or*

Rattle and Clinker, the half bred Dog and Terrier Bitch, hand-colored print from S. Alken, 1822 (Dr. Fleig's collection).

I. OLD FIGHTING DOG BREEDS

Bull and Terrier of the Viscount Purst, oil painting, circa 1830.

on foot . . . It is far livelier and agreeable than the breeds of dog from which it was bred, fit as before — but far, far more active — when it is a matter of making mischief . . . In comparison, the old Bulldog is a boring companion and the old terrier is not exactly distinguished by special size, nor is it as clever and ready for action. The modern crossbred dog combines all of these good traits, and also has an agreeable and temperamental character, without thereby — when encouraged — having lost the aggressiveness of its ancestors.

Wait a minute! The Bull and Terrier was a cross between the Bulldog and terrier, with a predominant infusion of terrier. It was bred for the fast dog fighting in the pit. Fights were divided into several rounds and often lasted more than an hour, as described in detail in *History of Fighting Dogs*. Its outward appearance and its character arise from the skillful combination of the good qualities of two old English dog breeds. It became extraordinarily popular and prized in England in the first half of the nineteenth century, because at that time a courageous dog that would fight to the death was greatly admired.

Of course, the survival of this newly created dog breed was also severely threatened by the banning of the fights in 1835. It turned out, however, that although bear and bull baiting soon disappeared through public regulation, dog fights continued to flourish in secret, and even increased underground due to the absence of other fights. Unfortunately, even in the twentieth century, it has still not been possible to eradicate this barbarism, which is so degrading to dog and man! These brave dogs thus continued to be abused by perverted people.

So the Bull and Terrier lived on. About the year 1860 the breed then split into two branches. James Hinks from Birmingham produced a pure-white Bull Terrier, in which only the name of the breed was retained. The colored and white forms that did not fit the standard of the new breed lived on for another 70 years in the dog pit, in a dark, or better said, blood-red illegality, until they finally were recognized as a legitimate dog breed in the Staffordshire Bull Terrier.

I admire particularly the wonderful painting by Sir Edwin Landseer, "Jack in Office," which we have in a print by G. Lewis. Jack is certainly a Bull and Terrier with a pronounced infusion of blood from the old Bulldog. Particularly characteristic is the sovereignty of this dog as "boss of the dog pack." A small king enthroned over his submissive subjects — an expression of the position of the Bull and Terrier in the English dog pack in 1830.

7. THE DANISH DOG

The title of this section is a provocation to all nationalistic supporters of the *Deutsche Dogge*. They have been angry for more than a hundred years that the Deutsche Dogge goes by the name *Great Dane* in England and many other countries, in the same way as the German Shepherd fanciers see red at the name *Alsatian*. In this book we do not concern ourselves with national pride or nationalistic prejudices, but rather of the historical truth.

It is historically documented that the systematic breeding of large dogs began very early in Denmark. The large Hunting Dog was combined with large Danish farm breeds, resulting in the wonderful Danish Dog. It is also historically true, however, that these large Danish Dog breeds themselves were no longer being supported by breeders in late nineteenth century Denmark, and were practically absorbed by the German dogge breeding stock. The Danish Dog thus died out in Denmark at the turn of the century; more precisely, it lives on in the Great Dane.

Back to the history of the large dogge breeds. Old paintings, sculpture, and prints are particularly compelling historical documents. In our discussion of the hunting of dangerous game, we presented a large number of artistic representations of heavy, long-legged dogge breeds hunting bears and boars in the Middle Ages.

The artistic renderings by Antonie Tempesta, Justus Sadler, Johann Elias Riedinger, Franz Snyders, Juriain Jacobsen are contemporary documents of the existence and appearance of old dogge breeds.

A very interesting engraving from Denmark, 1686 was created by Richard Blome and is dedicated loyally to His Highness George, Prince of

Sting, half-bred Terrier and Fox, Fox-terrier, from Stonehenge, 1859.

I. OLD FIGHTING DOG BREEDS

Jack in Office, engraving from Sir Edwin Landseer, circa 1830.

Boar hunt in Denmark, from Richard Blome, 1686.

I. OLD FIGHTING DOG BREEDS

Denmark. We see large, long-legged dogge breeds, which in head, build, and color already appear quite finished and would certainly appeal to any dogge fancier. Thus, dogge breeding in Denmark extends back to at least the seventeenth century.

We take an interesting reference to these dogs from the *Gentleman Farrier* of the year 1732. Here the *Danish Dog* is discussed as a large, short-haired dog breed. The usefulness of these dogs to their master is stressed. They are particularly suitable for carrying a lantern on the road, and they are easily trained to find a lost object many miles away on their own. The Danish Dog dependably protected the life and property of its master. In its company it is possible to sleep in total peace in a strange place; no one would dare to disturb the sleeping master and dog!

Interesting — and frequently completely misunderstood — is the account by Buffon (1707-1788) in his *Natural History of Four-legged Animals* about the Great Danish Dog. We take the following description from the original German edition of his work from the year 1785: *The Great Danish Dog (some also call it the Danish Coachdog because it likes to run behind the wagon, called the Danish Coachdog by some — Le grand Danois ou Danois de Carosse — Canis Daniae major). The dogs of this kind are considerably stronger in all parts of their body than the farm dogs. Apparently the only difference is their greater size. Their short coat is not uniform with respect to color. Most are fawn, others gray, some black, others marked with white gray, black, fawn and other blotches. Hunters give good reports on their usefulness, and, according to Mr. Pontoppidan's account, many of them are kept in Denmark . . .*

The Great Danish Dog, from Buffon, 1785.

Let us now examine Buffon's original illustration of *The Great Danish Dog*. It is surely beyond dispute that this male dog, standing in a courtly setting, is a good representative of the old Hunting Dog breeds. The heavy, broad skull with pronounced muzzle depth, powerful but short-backed and elegant build with long legs form a quite logical connection to the Hunting Dogs in the engravings of J. E. Riedinger.

With pleasure I return once more to our account of the Hunting Dog of the Middle Ages. We have previously demonstrated that this breed split into two forms corresponding to their purposes: a) large Hunting Dogs for hunting the bear and boar; b) smaller, heavier Bull Biters with shorter legs. In the *Great Danish Dog* we have a superb representative of the fast Hunting Dog. Buffon's illustration clearly shows a dog that, based on its anatomy, not only could trot alongside the coach but also knew how to fulfill its tasks in hunting dangerous game.

Edwards describes in the year 1800 in his *Cynographica Britannica* the Danish Dog as a breed of dog that should be considered as falling approximately between the Greyhound and the Mastiff. The shoulder height of this dog ranges between 28 and 31 inches. The head is carried upright, the muzzle is quite prominent, and the ears are cropped. He speaks of a deep chest with a narrow body, long, straight, and powerful legs, and a thin tail. Edwards admires a particularly beautiful color variety in the Harlequin Dane, a dog with large and small blotches on a white background. He reports further that the Danish Dog usually runs alongside the coach as a wagon dog, where the powerful interplay of its muscles, the fluid gait, and the powerful gallop are a delight to see. Its appearance contributes considerably to the pomp of the nobility and wealthy. As the ideal of the nobility, Edwards names the coach accompanied by a pair of noble Harlequin Dogs. Thus, the dogge was already considered a renowned dog this early on! This is not surprising when we see the superb illustrations in Edwards's *Book of Fast, Noble Dogs*, which surely were a pleasure to behold for any animal lover. What a contrast to the earlier view of molossoid dogs, which were supposed to be as ugly and frightening as possible! There is a world of difference between this noble Danish Dog and the old, coarse Hunting Dogs and Bull Biters!

The Danish Dog, Syd Edwards, 1800.

In his account from the year 1845, Colonel Smith makes a clear distinction between the old boar dogs distributed throughout Germany and the Danish Dog. The Boar Dog was not nearly as large as the Danish Dog and was particularly widespread in southern and eastern Germany.

Richardson describes the breed in 1845 in his dog book *The Danish Dog* as the largest existing dog breed in the world. These dogs are the *most useful destroyers of wolves and boars*. As a rule, these dogs had a shoulder height of more than 30 inches. The skull was broad above the eyes, the lateral cranial bones were broad and distinguished this dog breed from the true Mastiff. The main difference to the Mastiff consisted of the much elongated muzzle; the flews were also not as loose and did not hang as low. Purebred Danish Dogs were short haired, their tail thin and carried low, the neck slightly arched, the ears small

I. OLD FIGHTING DOG BREEDS

and drooping by nature. The ears of these dogs, however, were always cropped in the puppy stage.

Stonehenge, whom we are indebted to for Richardson's description, adds that the Great Dane was used in Denmark and Norway for elk hunting. He illustrates the description of the breed with an engraving by L. Wells from the year 1859.

From numerous documents we can prove that in the middle of the nineteenth century large dogge breeds also arose in many German states. The old Hunting Dog was a capable foundation for successful dogge breeding. In Württemberg a broad breeding stock arose, and soon gained a good reputation as the "Ulm Dogge." The districts of Hamburg, Schleswig Holstein, and Berlin also became early centers of independent dogge breeding. We should keep in mind that Germany did not emerge as a unified nation until 1870, that only afterwards could a certain degree of cooperation extend across the borders of the former states, that not until then was it possible to speak of the Great Dane. There is no doubt that the north-German dogge breeding was influenced to an extraordinary degree by breeding stock imported from Denmark.

Strebel sees the origin of the Great Dane in a large meeting of breeders in 1878. However, the Deutsche Doggen Club e. V. was not established until ten years later, on January 12, 1888 in Berlin. It was the first German

Great Dane, from Stonehenge, engraving by L. Wells, 1859.

association for purebred dogs. Since then the breeding of the Great Dane has been systematically directed and promoted by this club.

Let us now take leave of the Danish Dog. It had a fate similar to that of the Bull and Terrier, in that its actual heyday began only in the breeding of the Great Dane, just as the Bull and Terrier found its perfection in the Bull Terrier. The close relationship of the Great Dane breed to the Danish Dog is apparent in the original illustration by Friedrich Specht, which was published in 1874 in *Diana — Blätter für Jagd- und Hundefreunde.* Here we encounter once more this exquisite breed of dog in an appropriate courtly setting. The illustration in *Diana* stands out as the absolutely true to nature portrayal of the Danish Dog. Fitzinger states in the accompanying description of the breed that the Danish Dog is the most beautiful of all large and strong dog breeds. *And as the lion is given the*

Danish Dog, illustration by Friedrich Specht, 1874.

I. OLD FIGHTING DOG BREEDS

name of king of the animals, the Danish Dog could lay claim to such a name among the dogs.

8. THE CHINCHA BULLDOG

It may seem strange to my readers at first to be confronted with an old dog breed that the overwhelming majority of all dog lovers have never heard of, whose name even dog experts very often are unfamiliar with. The only evidence of this dog breed is a series of finds — dog mummies, old skeletons, and ceramic figures. What is it doing in a book about breeds of fighting dogs?

There is scientific evidence that these old skeletons and the ceramic figures prove the existence of a long since extinct breed of dog from ancient Peru, from a time long before the arrival of Europeans in this land, hence long before Pizarro destroyed the ancient Incan culture in 1533.

I readily admit that I present the Chincha Bulldog in my book because it offers clear proof that — as previously stated in another place — in many places in the world dog breeds have

Head of the Chincha Bulldog, Chimu figure, circa 1200 A.D.

arisen completely independently of one another, purely on the basis of their utility. Even so, these dog breeds resemble one another so closely that we simply assume at first that they must be related to one another. Peru was first discovered by Europeans in the sixteenth century. Nonetheless, long before this discovery there existed here a breed of dog with all the signs of being related to the English Bulldog. Professors Max Hilzheimer and Richard N. Wegner in the year 1937 studied scientifically these mummified dogs and excavated skeletons in 1937. They discovered, surprisingly, that the skull of the Chincha Bulldog shared a wealth of similarities with the skull of the French Bulldog of the twentieth century. Moreover, there were similarities, not only between the skulls, but between the entire anatomies as well.

First let me present the Chincha Bulldog in a head portrait of a Chimu sculpture. This piece was collected on the Frankfurt Bolivian expedition of 1927-1929. It comes from the ruins of a town in Trujillo in northern Peru.

The original Indian inhabitants of Peru have left behind a wealth of animal and human ceramic figures. There is little scientific doubt that they are accurate portrayals of nature. We are indebted to the same expedition for a sitting figure of this dog breed. It comes from the locality of Pacasmayo in northern Peru. Both statues are of so-called *black Chimu-ware*.

The amazing thing is that in the excavations of the burial grounds of Ancon in central Peru, the mummified bodies of dogs, as well as skulls and skeletons, were found. These are superbly preserved and confirm unambiguously that bulldog-like dogs lived in Peru in the period from 1100 to 1470 A.D. They are identical to the ceramic figures.

Sitting Chincha Bulldog, black Chimu-ware, circa 1200 A.D.

In the *Zeitschrift für Hundeforschung, vol. VI*, from the year 1937, Hilzheimer and Wegner demonstrate a downright astounding similarity in the skulls found in Peru and skulls of a modern French Bulldog. Mind you, these are precise scientific comparisons of actual dog skulls, comparisons of the individual cranial bones, the tooth position, the cavities, and so forth.

Using the ceramic figures, the superbly preserved dog mummies, and the skeletons, the scientists described the Chincha Bulldog as a small, elongated, low-slung dog with a broad chest, lightly bent front legs, and a medium-length tail. It had a large head with a pear-shaped cranium and a strongly set off, very short facial part of the skull. The nose was normal or may have been a double nose. The eyes were protruding and the ears were large and displaced to the side—so-called bat ears. The lower jaw had an undershot bite with a well turned up front part of the lower jaw.

Now I must make a necessary clarification. The existing ceramic figures do not permit a precise determination of the exact type of bite of the Chincha Bulldog. They neither confirm an undershot nor an overshot bite. Professors Hilzheimer and Wegner explained this by pointing out that the Indian artists certainly were no zoologists and also had no intention of making a cynological model. The clear proof of the undershot bite in this Peruvian dog breed lies in the skull finds, whereby ten different finds were evaluated by 1936.

On the basis of all artwork and skeletal finds, this Indian dog in ancient Peru resembles the French Bulldog to a striking degree. Certainly it is important, however, to emphasize a decisive difference determined from the comparative examination of the skulls. The skull of the French Bulldog is virtually identical with that of the Chincha Bulldog in the facial area. The cranium, however, displays a very clear difference. The cranium of the Chincha Bulldog is pear shaped, but spherical in the French Bulldog. From this it can be inferred that the Chincha Bulldog is not the dwarf form of an original, larger dog. As is generally known, dwarf forms and an apple-shaped cranium are closely linked. From this we can conclude that the Chincha Bulldog was a small breed of dog from the start.

Unfortunately, this Indian Bulldog is extinct. We have yet to find any clear artistic or written references to the purposes of this dog in ancient Peru. We know from other finds, however, that a medium-sized hunting dog lived in Peru at the same time. Was the Chincha Bulldog the house dog of the original inhabitants of Peru, as, for example, the French Bulldog is with us today? But why would a house dog need the undershot bite? Was it a fighting dog after all? For the moment the question must remain unanswered. Maybe science will help us to answer this question some day.

II. MODERN FIGHTING DOG BREEDS

Determining which of today's dog breeds belong to the group of fighting dogs is not an easy task. Many a reader will be surprised to find dogs like the Pug or the Boston Terrier in this group of breeds, which he would more likely have classified with the lap dogs. Others will ask why the various breeds of working dog are not included here, since they "battle" today in various sporting competitions. Then I await the question of why we do not include the Saint Bernard—Alpine Mastiff—or the Newfoundland! The group of "fighting dog breeds" is regarded as elite among the dog breeds—naturally, everyone wants to have a share of the valor!

We must distinguish for what purpose a breed was created. It must be grouped according to the ancestors of the dog, according to the foundation breeds. Accordingly, I have largely been directed by the influence of the old fighting dog breeds on modern dog breeding. The large breeds of watchdog and herding dog certainly belong to the sheepdog group. I consider the Saint Bernard in its systematic breeding as a rescue dog to have been influenced by the Mastiff, but this does not make it a fighting dog. Size is not a determining factor for membership in or exclusion from the circle of fighting dogs. In the first book we of course saw how often the smallest dogs were misused as fighting dogs.

Yes, I will emphasize this once more. Fighting against other animals or dogs is a barbaric abuse of the dog. If we can understand why it existed in the Middle Ages on the basis of wars, hunting, and social disturbance, in modern times clear laws exist in most civilized countries that penalize the abuse of the dog by spiritually disturbed people.

Nonetheless, the knowledge of the common past of the dog breeds collected in this book is of great value to the dog fancier. We have already proved in individual cases how intensely the anatomy and character of the dog are influenced by the range of tasks for which this breed of dog was bred. We can use this knowledge to understand the nature of our dogs. We also find an explanation for certain body forms, which at first glance appear ugly, revolting, inappropriate, or sick.

Many dog fanciers prize the unique character of the old fighting dog. It is a self-confident, independent dog, completely unsuitable for those dog fanciers who demand a kind of slavish obedience from their fellow man. Only a person who is secure in his own identity will succeed with a dog that prefers to lead its own life alongside man. This demands human respect. We must display tolerance and understanding for the personality of the dog.

I therefore ask that you not misunderstand the inclusion of a number of modern dog breeds under the rubric "modern fighting dog breeds." I have no intention of implying by this that they stand ready to return to the pit, should the old fights happen to be revived in the present century. Also, do not be misled by those false prophets who encourage such fights as a way to test and preserve the unique character of these dogs. Today we have enough information from behavioral research to guide the breeder in selecting the right animals to breed to produce good dogs that truly belong to our time.

Now let us go on to the individual breeds.

1. TIBETAN MASTIFF

If we take a look at the photograph that portrays the modern Tibetan Mastiff, it is clear that this dog is virtually identical to the old Tibetan Dog that we came to know in the historical part of the book. It is an imposing male, strong boned, full of substance, without being overloaded in the slightest, with a nearly ideal head, luxuriant coat—an exquisite breed of dog. I believe that many a fancier of large dogs would be inspired by the true Tibetan Mastiff. For that reason, I have also included a picture of the puppies bred from this male in 1981 in Germany. They were photographed at three weeks of age.

Tibetan Mastiff puppies, three weeks old, 1981, bred by Böse, Remscheid.

The brighter the light, the deeper the shadow! Throughout the twentieth century it has been and continues to be extraordinarily difficult to breed this dog in its homeland, the Tibetan highlands. The reasons for this include tremendous political confusion and a social upheaval of the population. The Dalai Lama was forced to leave his medieval religious state, along with a group of his subjects. Today the Dalai Lama lives in exile in India. Many Tibetans left with him and became settled craftsmen instead of livestock-tending nomads. Scarcely a Tibetan Mastiff survived the exodus from its homeland.

As early as 1903, Drury, in *British Dogs*, called for giving this splendid breed of dog a new home in England. He expected that "the famous English art of dog breeding" would cultivate the Tibetan Mastiff. Surprisingly, the imported animals, if they even survived the month-long and extraordinarily hard voyage to England, were kept primarily in zoos. Not only acclimation problems of a medical sort made dogs and breeding stock hard to obtain, apparently the adjustment to the English environment also proved to be extremely difficult. Numerous accounts state that as they grew older these Tibetans became such a danger to their civilized surroundings that they were presented to zoos as a gift. Behind iron bars, they were marveled and gawked at as if they were exotic predators.

Attempts to breed them failed because the dogs either did not mate at all or their puppies died from various illnesses. These inhabitants of the high mountains did not tolerate emotionally or psychically the move from high altitudes of about 4000 meters across the ocean to England, to other European countries or to the United States.

Dr. Mary Täuber writes in 1979 on this subject in *Unser Rassehund (Our Pedigree Dog)*: *Direct imports from Tibet generally do not stay healthy for long and usually are unable to breed. Lower altitudes cause disturbances in circulation and put a strain on the heart. Even Sikkim and Nepal are not tolerated by some. The dogs become dull and lethargic. The undercoat is strongly hydrophilic, so that in damp weather it can be downright wrung out. The result is rheumatic disease, kidney damage, and virulent eczema. So far it has not been possible to keep the offspring of dogs*

II. Modern Fighting Dog Breeds

Male Tibetan Mastiff, *Tü-Bo,* original import from Tibet in the late 1970s.

imported directly from Tibet alive for long. This has been possible, however, with dogs that have become acclimated over several generations to a transitional climate such as in Sikkim or Nepal. Not a particularly encouraging outlook for the passionate breeder!

I find a photograph from the 1930s interesting and impressive, a head study of the male dog Tomtru imported to England directly from Tibet. It is excellent proof of the independence and unmistakable type of this breed. In any event, we learn from England that even in this country many attempts to breed the Tibetan Mastiff failed, despite the famous English art of dog breeding.

Today there exist very few true purebred specimens of this ancient dog breed. It would not be wrong to say that it is even threatened with extinction. It has long been lamented that the Mastiffs brought down to the Indian foothills lose their type and health rather quickly. All the more interesting is an account by Mrs. Hedy Nouc from the year 1980, published in *Unser Rassehund (Our Pedigree Dog)*, about an expedition to find the Tibetan Mastiff in the Himalayas (not identical with the true Tibetan highlands!). With the support of the Indian officials it was possible, near a small group of houses named Palamper at 3000 meters above sea level, to assemble 42 Tibetan Mastiffs and the large herds of sheep and goats entrusted to them. This was a unique opportunity to gain a realistic overview of the state of the remnants of this old breed of dog.

Each of the large herds was accompanied by one to three Mastiffs. Their task was less to drive the goats and sheep but to protect the herds from predators. Bears and leopards threaten the herds in the Himalayas. When they arrived in Palamper, the Europeans had already traveled one day by jeep and hiked seven miles, surmounting an altitude change of 1200 meters. The extreme temperatures they measured in May were about 30° C during the day and about 0°C at night.

Hedy Nouc considers the term Tibetan Mastiff to be merely a collective concept. The shepherds distinguished between the black dogs of the Bara-Bengali type and black-and-tan Bharmouri dogs (black with tan markings). In addition, there were golden Mastiffs of the Lahauli type. The encounter with these guardians of the herds was impressive: *And then the first herds poured in from all directions. I will never forget this moment. Herds of sheep, mixed with the Indian and above all Tibetan goats. The shepherds with their picturesque head coverings and one to three Mastiffs with each herd.*

Mrs. Nuoc describes these herding dogs as large, powerful animals with a strong, straight back and feathered legs. *In these regions, any dog with a faulty backbone, hips, or hindquarters could not survive. The shepherds with their herds and the accompanying dogs must be able to move here as dancers on the tight rope.*

She emphasizes very strongly the peaceful disposition of the dogs, the little aggression displayed toward others of their kind, the resistance toward the people only when they approached to herd entrusted to the dog. The dogs were fed a kind of flat bread, accompanied by cornmeal and goat's or sheep's milk. None of the animals made a feeble impression. They had powerful bites, mostly scissors, a few level, none undershot. None of the 42 dogs showed any sign of skin problems.

The big surprise for the passionate breeder: Of the thirteen best male dogs encountered, ten were neutered! In general the dogs were about 66 centimeters at the shoulder, but the neutered dogs were significantly larger and more powerful. Mrs. Nouc raises the question of whether the frequent castration of the males is the explanation for the repeatedly reported *gigantic growth of the Tibetans*. Scientists describe this sort of thing as *eunuchoid hypergrowth*. Castration before sexual maturity extends the growth of the large bones of the extremities in particular. According to the testimony of the shepherds, the fairly regular castration of the male dogs tending the herds is necessary because only in this way do the males stay dependably with the herds. Sooner or later the others disappear into the wilderness in search of females.

And so it turned out that on this Tibetan encounter a kind of dog show was held. First prize, a handsome Merino ram, went to the owner of a rather mediocre male dog. The most attractive male was ineligible because it was neutered. After the dog show the proceedings took a decidedly European turn: the owner of the most beautiful—castrated—male dog drowned his sorrows in alcohol!

The standard of the Tibetan Mastiff requires a shoulder height of about 65

II. MODERN FIGHTING DOG BREEDS

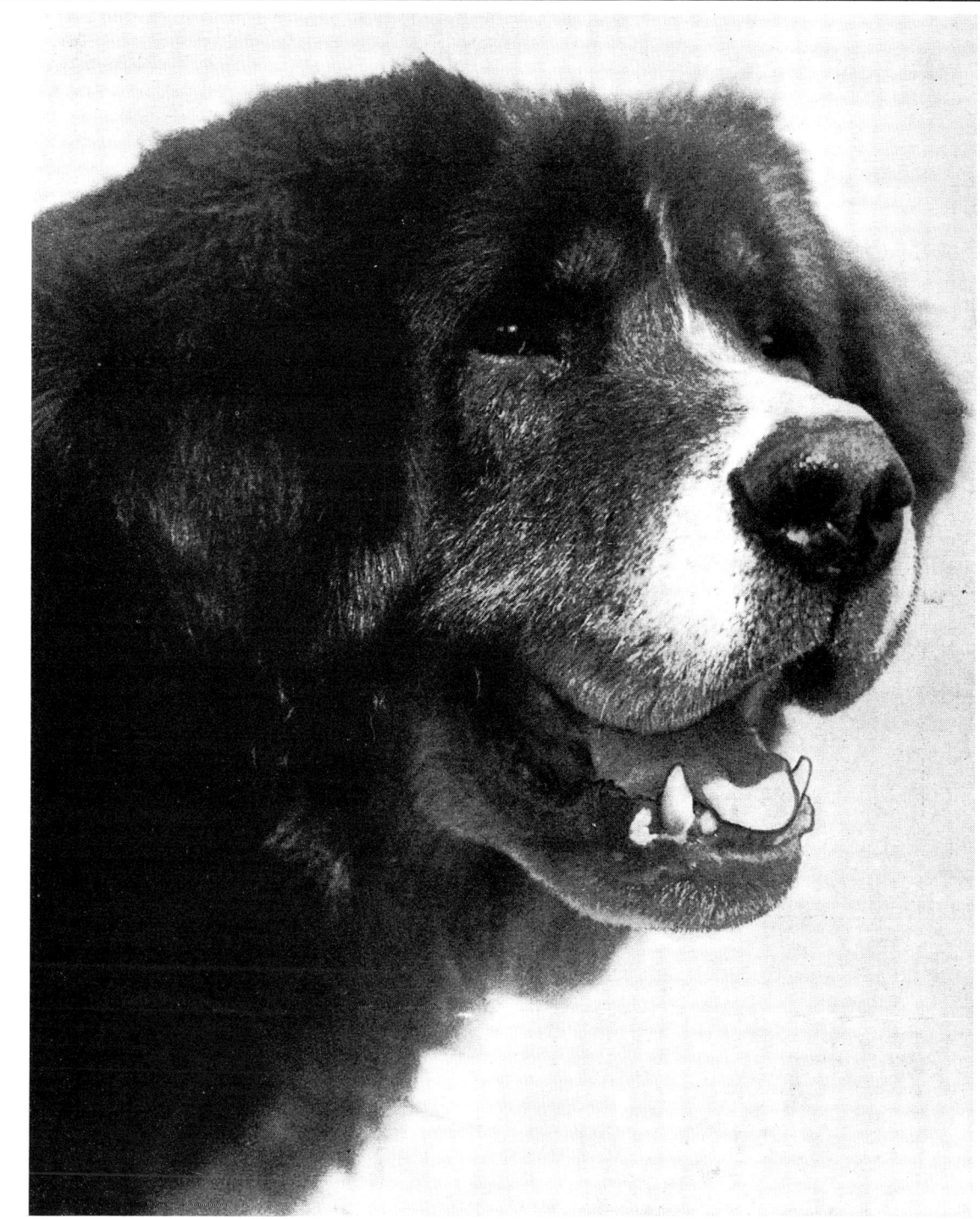

Head study of the Tibetan Mastiff, *Tomtru*, circa 1930, original import from England.

centimeters and a weight of approximately 50 kilograms. It is true that the Tibetan Mastiff is a rather atypical fighting dog. Its only purpose is to protect the herd from predators. We know that this ancient breed could be one of the roots of all fighting dog breeds, and in the past was also frequently used as a war dog. The Tibetan Mastiff is a first-class protector of the herd, house, and family. The large yak herds of Tibet have been replaced today in the Himalayas by goats and sheep. These more peaceful charges have also changed the duties of this herding dog.

I first encountered Tü-Bo at a big dog show in Belgium. I had the opportunity there to examine the male dog very thoroughly in the waiting period before the judging. Frankly speaking, I felt somewhat groggy because of the numerous serious anatomical faults I had found in the other molossoid dogs in the show. This made my encounter with Tü-Bo all the more impressive. As I used my eyes and probing hands to examine the anatomy of the compact, large-framed, powerful dog, I asked myself why it should not be possible after all to preserve this fundamentally sound dog breed. Finally a large-framed molossoid dog that was not overloaded with excess body weight! Despite its power, the dog had a fundamentally sound anatomy. Admittedly, I generously overlooked the fact that the angulation of its hindquarters could have been more perfect, its movement from the rear more forceful. Nonetheless, this dog breed should be able to move freely. After all, it is entrusted with protecting the herds. The dog has a solid anatomy and also exhibits the typical self-confident temperament of the old fighting dog.

I realize that very little pure breeding stock exists outside of its homeland. Imports from the United States are questionable in regard to anatomy and temperament. Nonetheless, I think it is high time to do something to save this splendid old dog breed.

I can think of only one promising way to proceed: namely to go up to the old homeland of the breed, to carefully screen the last remaining representatives of these Tibetans, and to rebuild the dog breed systematically in a suitable environment in a peaceful country.

Allow me to fantasize a little more. Why could the breed not find a new home, experience a rebirth, in the European Alps, perhaps in the same way the splendid Saint Bernard was created at the Hospice of St. Bernard? Travel has become much faster today and veterinary medicine could contribute to making such transport relatively harmless to the dogs. The technique of artificial insemination also would be more than useful for managing and improving the breed. The raw mountain climate of Central Europe could not be so different from the accustomed climate in Tibet that insurmountable difficulties would be expected here. Over the years these dogs could then slowly manage the descent to the foothills and then the valleys, without endangering their health! We have the responsibility in the late twentieth century to preserve for our descendants the animals and plants threatened by our civilization. We do this with threatened wild animals and plants, so why not with the Tibetan Mastiff, one of the oldest breeds of dog in the world? This breed surely deserves to live on, to flourish again in its old, imposing form!

Can something like this only be accomplished by the state and its officials? Why could the sympathy and responsibility of breeders not do the

II. MODERN FIGHTING DOG BREEDS

Tibetan Mastiffs in the Himalayas, 1979, Nouc expedition.

same for our dogs? We should come up with something soon to save this splendid dog breed from extinction!

2. MASTIFF

In the first part of this book, we left the Mastiff at the turn of the century. Sydney Turner, the greatest old Mastiff man and founding member of the Old English Mastiff Club, had urgently warned against breeding only for Mastiff heads, instead of carefully and conscientiously considering the total anatomy of the dog. From his encyclopedia we show a head study of the famous Ch. Crown Prince, whelped in 1880. This was the ideal which led to the overweighing of the head type in English breeding. Crown Prince became—particularly through his daughters—the power of change. Anything that did not correspond to this ideal of a Mastiff head was viewed by judges and breeders as second class, regardless of how good the total anatomy of the dog was. The new ideal had one-third muzzle and two-thirds forehead, with a pronounced stop. The old lines with a longer muzzle, even the famous Lyme Hall line, were no longer in demand. The warnings of responsible cynologists were thrown to the wind.

We will encounter similar head fetishes in many other dog breeds. Although it is true that the dog's head in truly important for the breed type in virtually all breeds of dog in the world, it is equally true, as the famous Tom Horner once told me, that *The dog doesn't run on his head!* If all dog breeders would only realize this! The perfect head is no doubt the crowning touch, and it should be fostered in champion dogs. But the perfect dog's head can never replace the proper basic anatomy of the dog! After all, what good is a crowned head without a body to put it on? Very noble!

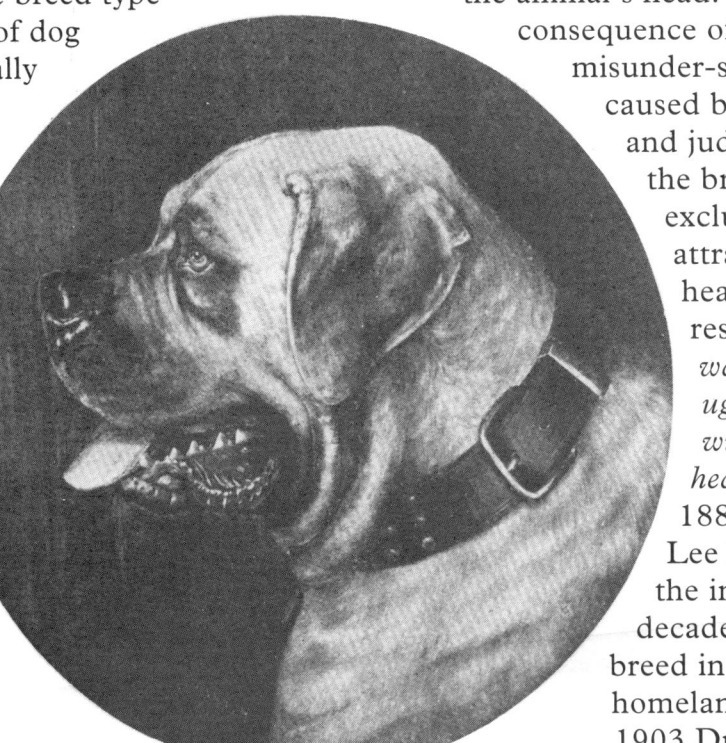

Head study of the Mastiff, *Ch. Crown Prince*, from 1880.

As early as 1889 Hugh Dalziel concluded that movement in the Mastiff often left something to be desired. This applied particularly to weakness in the hindquarters, which often revealed itself as a cow-hocked stance in the standing position. It suffered from weak musculature in the hindquarters, steep angulation, and an overly long, soft back. He denounces the recent breeding of quite fleshy dogs, instead of ones with real substance. This led to the loss of symmetry and mobility in the breed. With these Mastiffs you no longer had the sense that they were once bred as true war dogs. They were now surely fit only for garrison duty after a lost war.

William Wade criticized in 1891 that of approximately one hundred requirements in the standard for the Mastiff about forty referred to details of the animal's head. A consequence of misunder-standings caused by the club and judges was the breeding exclusively for attractive heads. The result was *waddling, ugly monsters with a dream head!* In 1889 Randon Lee lamented the increasing decadence of the breed in its homeland. In 1903 Drury stressed: *A breeder of the Mastiff in any case cannot afford to neglect even the smallest detail in breeding.* The question was, would breeders ever understand this?

A Mr. Smith, an ardent admirer of this old breed of dog, wrote for the magazine *Country Life*. He reported about the Mastiff a number of times between the years 1914 and 1928. In 1914 he interviewed Colonel Walker, a pioneer of the breed since 1875. This man lamented a clear loss of quality in the breed beginning at the turn of the century, brought about by foolish breeding according to the latest fashion. He claimed that, in the year 1914, there was scarcely a good Mastiff left in the

II. MODERN FIGHTING DOG BREEDS

Head study of a modern Mastiff, England, 1982, *Bellabees Blunder of Bredmardine*.

Tibetan Mastiff. Photo by Isabelle Francais.

whole country.

I find it ironic that we owe the existence of the wonderful old fighting dog breeds to war, in which war dogs were once a necessity, but that virtually all the old breeds of large fighting dogs fell victim to war. The two World Wars of the twentieth century did not need war dogs in the former sense, but only as ambulance dogs and message carriers. These wars had access to totally new killing machines, and the bravest war dog of ancient pedigree could no longer protect his people against these weapons.

The Mastiff, once "the war dog par excellence," was reduced to being a "useless mouth to feed" in the terrible wars of the twentieth century, because it competed for meager rations with starving people around the world. It is a painful fact that the old Mastiff nearly died out because of the two World Wars. The large, heavy dog breeds probably had the hardest time surviving these bitter, hungry times. They had become superfluous for war, replaced by shells, poison gas, bombs, tanks, airplanes . . .

During World War I the breeding of the Mastiff in Britain came almost to a standstill. On June 11, 1921, our Mr. Smith reported in *Country Life* that scarcely a Mastiff could be found at the newly revived larger dog shows. The breed now had very few fanciers. Furthermore, at least half the remaining animals were miserable in character and were hardly an advertisement for the breed. The few good Mastiffs in Britain could be counted on the fingers of one hand.

Starting in about 1925, the breed experienced a marked recovery. It attracted more and more fanciers, who made it their life's work to breed good Mastiffs. C. R. Oliver (Menai kennel), Mr. and Mrs. L. Scheerboom (Havengore kennel), Mr. and Mrs. Oliver (Hellingly), and Norman Haigh (Ashenhurst) were only a few of the notable breeders. The largest Mastiff kennel during these years was Hellingly. We illustrate the fruits of the hard work expended in bringing the breed back to a high standard in 1931 with the famous Ch. Ajax of Hellingly. This male dog had a very positive influence on the history of the breed. We show the very imposing form of this dog in profile and in a head study. Ajax is said to have weighed about 90 kilograms.

Unfortunately, the breeding of attractive Mastiffs was abruptly broken off with the outbreak of war in 1939.

How badly Mastiff breeding in Britain was affected by this war is shown by a newspaper story from the United States. *The Atlanta Journal* reported on August 11, 1940—the war in Europe was not yet a year old—that Atlanta was increasingly becoming a haven for imperiled, noble English pedigree dogs. Two exquisite Mastiffs had just arrived in town. Mrs. King had inquired of the five leading English Mastiff kennels whether they wished to send their dogs to the United States. Four of the five kennels had already given away all their dogs because the food necessary to maintain a responsible Mastiff kennel was impossible to obtain. Mrs. Bowles had managed to keep two Mastiffs, Remus and Prunella, in the London area. Before these animals arrived in Atlanta, they had to live for months on toast and vegetables. By the time they reached the United States, they had lost more than fifty pounds of their normal weight.

The post-war situation of Mastiff breeding in Britain can be documented on the basis of the minutes of the Old English Mastiff Club. The first meeting

II. MODERN FIGHTING DOG BREEDS

Male Mastiff, *Ch. Ajax of Hellingly*, 1931.

since 1939 took place on October 20, 1946. During World War II, dog shows and club life for all dog breeds was practically extinguished in Britain. Fifteen members came to this meeting in 1946. Their main concern was to save the Mastiff. The first census for all of Britain showed the existence of only 20 living animals, nearly all of them too old to be eligible for breeding. A serious distemper epidemic led to even more losses. By late 1947, only seven Mastiffs were counted in Britain. The end of the old breed was at hand!

There was a male dog named Taurus. Because its owner had been killed in a bombing attack its precise pedigree was unknown to the Mastiff breeders. Three well-known special judges from The Kennel Club declared him to be a purebred Mastiff, so he was registered in the stud book by The Kennel Club, naturally with the entries "sire and dam unknown." It subsequently was determined that Taurus was descended from a cross between a Mastiff and a Bullmastiff. This Taurus probably was the only surviving virile stud dog in Britain. He was bred to the bitch Sally of Coldblow, whose bloodline was influenced strongly by the old Havengore line. This mating produced Nydia of Frithend. This bitch became the new milestone in the further development of Mastiff breeding in Britain following World War II.

Mrs. Dickin, the secretary of the Old English Mastiff Club, flew to the United

II. MODERN FIGHTING DOG BREEDS

Mastiff. Photo by Isabelle Francais.

States in 1947. Despite the earlier export of many good Mastiffs to that country, here too Mastiff breeding was at rock bottom. Her hopes of reestablishing the breed in Britain by importing good dogs were dashed, and she returned—dogless—from the United States.

At this point allow me to quote from Marie Antoinette Moore from her Mastiff book that was published in 1978. I realize that her sober observations hit home with the passionate Mastiff devotee, but they speak the truth. *In actuality, the ancient history of Mastiff breeding is absolutely of secondary importance for the Mastiff of today. The ancient breed of the Mastiff was nearly extinct at the end of World War II.*

It is certainly a bitter truth to say farewell to such a glorious past. Not many Mastiff breeders are prepared to admit that by 1947 this breed lay in ruins, upon which alone this dog breed could not have been built up again. It turned out to be possible to rebuild the breed after all, but many compromises had to be made to achieve this success. On the other hand, I think the farewell to the glorious past is somewhat of an exaggeration. We have seen many times in this book that there is a close inner relationship between all the breeds of fighting dog, that the histories of these dog breeds are interconnected.

Although Taurus, the crossbreed between Mastiff and Bullmastiff, was the first cornerstone of the rebuilding process after the war, virtually all authors will admit off the record that in these first post-war years the rebirth of the Mastiff breed was possible only because of the infusion of new blood from other large-framed dog breeds. Great Danes, Bullmastiffs, Saint Bernards, and Newfoundlands contributed to the rebirth of the Mastiff.

You could say that these breeds now gave back to the Mastiff what they had taken from the breed in the first place. This again reveals the inner relationship between the great, old family of fighting dogs.

Even in very recent times, we can see clear indications of active incrossing in the outward appearance of Mastiff puppies. We observe repeatedly, for example, that purebred litters include puppies with fairly long to long hair. There is talk of a recessive gene, and we do not really know how it entered the breed. Was it a true mutation? Of course many Saint Bernards and Newfoundlands are supposed to have this gene. Douglas B. Oliff writes in *Molosser Magazine* in 1982 that he himself has seen a puppy from a purebred mating with distinct pied markings, such as occur in the Saint Bernard. These color variations are revealed as distinct shading within the regions of brown color. He also saw Mastiff puppies with distinct Newfoundland-type fur. At the Crufts dog show in 1982, I myself saw a very attractive, large-framed Mastiff. Its head, expression, and coat, however, clearly called to mind a Leonberger. There can scarcely be any reasonable doubt that the Mastiff was rebuilt after World War II only through secret borrowing from other large dog breeds. Moreover, this is by no means the only breed of dog with foreign blood pulsing in its veins. We will return to this discussion at a later point.

In 1949 the Old English Mastiff Club received a donation of two Mastiff puppies from British Columbia, Canada. Both were descended from the old Havengore-Hellingly lines. These dogs proved to be particularly valuable for rebuilding the breed after they were bred to Nydia's offspring. At the end of

II. MODERN FIGHTING DOG BREEDS

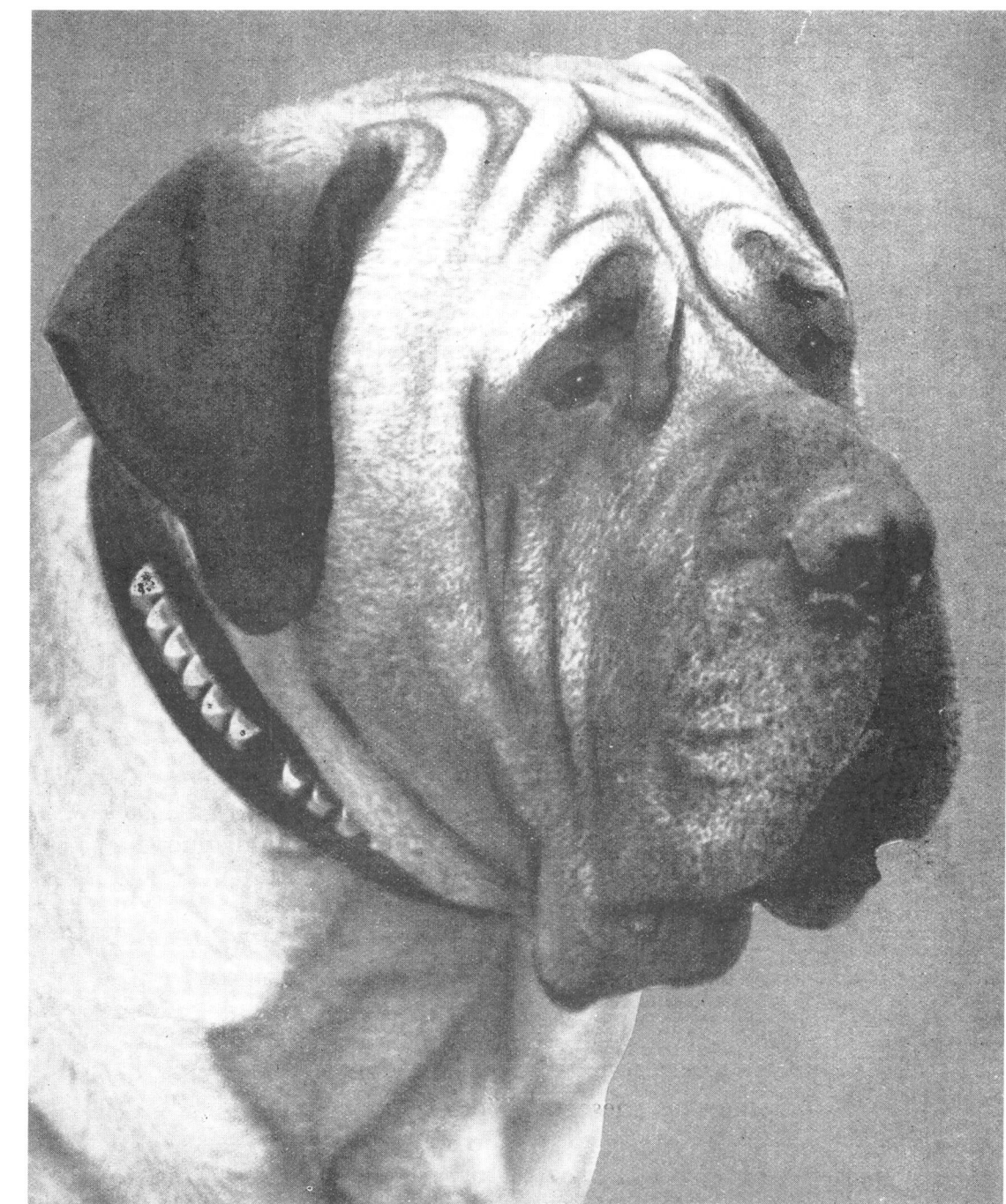

Head study of *Ch. Ajax of Hellingly*, 1931.

1949 there were only 15 Mastiffs in Britain, but by 1950 there were 50. The breed had gained a foothold again.

Of course, the breeders now had to overcome two problems. On the one hand stood the old, pure Mastiff lines, burdened with a very high coefficient of inbreeding and with correspondingly obvious symptoms of degeneration. Serious faults in temperament, such as shyness and extreme nervousness, can be traced back to this inbreeding, and even today are encountered far too often in the breed. On the other hand, the incrossing produced continual setbacks, which corrupted the strived-for breed type. Moreover, the demand for Mastiffs was so strong in the 1950s, that—putting it mildly—there were fewer good dogs to breed. The urgently necessary selection was ignored, and the faults became entrenched in the breed.

Although the United States held the better cards after the war, the breeding of top Mastiffs gradually shifted back to the motherland. A number of breeders deserve special mention: Mrs. Scheerboom rebuilt her kennel (Havengore); Mrs. Dickin, a club member since 1922, secretary since 1933, president of the club in 1966 and 1967, made use of her many years of experience in her kennel, Goring. Miss Bell, a breeder since 1923, led the Withybush Mastiffs to success after success after the war. Unfortunately, in her will she ordered that all her Mastiffs more than two years old be destroyed after her death. She did this to spare her dogs the trouble of a move—and dealt a serious blow to the slowly recovering dog breed! Mrs. Lindley's Copenore kennel bred over 200 puppies and clear line breeding produced 15 self-bred champions.

Overall, breeding had gained strength in Britain. Douglas B. Oliff points out that it is a miracle that the Mastiff existed again, and that we are indebted to all the breeders who contributed to saving this breeding from a nearly hopeless situation. We show the modern Mastiff of desirable type in the accompanying illustrations.

Mastiff, *Ch. Forefoot Prince Igor of Bredmardine, Mastiff of the Year* in England in 1979 and 1980.

Now a few important comments on the standard of the Mastiff. All authors are unanimous in stressing that reaching the desired size is the ultimate goal of breeding with this large dog. This goal, however, must never be achieved through longer leg bones but through the proportional enlargement of the dog's entire anatomy. All authors unanimously reject greater shoulder height at the expense of substance and proper proportions. Accordingly, the large-framed, substantial Mastiff is the desired goal.

Furthermore, I found unanimous agreement among experts that exaggerated breeding for individual anatomical points always leads to grave faults and must not be tolerated. Authors stress repeatedly that this large dog, despite its impressive substance, must be flexible with firmly knit tendons and muscles. Steep angulation and weaknesses in the forequarters or

II. MODERN FIGHTING DOG BREEDS

hindquarters are faults.

A look in the show ring in the 1980s documents that it is very difficult to attain all these goals. Unfortunately, I have determined time after time that the dogs are the most imposing and beautiful when they are lying down. When standing they display a number of faults: a substantial percentage of the animals are overbuilt, the fronts and rears exhibit weaknesses in the tendons, and the angulation is often far from the old ideal. All these faults become even more glaring, of course, when the dog is in full motion.

The Englishman has a basic requirement for a dog breed: the dogs must be sound. This term is not equivalent to healthy; it is more properly interpreted as the striving for an "anatomically correct build." It goes without saying that this is particularly hard to achieve precisely with our large and substantial dog breeds. All our dogs are descended from the wolf, a running predator. It seems obvious that we must not overload the anatomy of such a running predator with oversized bones and an excessive abundance of substance. Otherwise, the muscles and tendons will simply be overburdened. This is a basic physical law, which dog breeders, for all their hand-wringing, cannot change. One author has warned against "elephantism" in the breeding of large dogs. I am in complete agreement

Imposing even when lying down. Mastiffs in Germany, 1981. Here we can see the calm majesty of this breed.

Head study of the Mastiff, *Bredmardine Beelzebub*, 21 months old.

II. MODERN FIGHTING DOG BREEDS

with this. The English standard for the Mastiff recognizes no minimum shoulder height. In the United States, the standard requires at least 30 inches in male dogs and 27.5 inches in bitches. A male dog of this size weighs about 80 kilograms, a bitch about 64 kilograms. Since breeding dogs with longer legs is missing the point, dispensing with a height requirement, as in Britain, seems the better solution.

It is surprising that on the Continent—with the possible exception of the Netherlands—the Mastiff always had a hard time winning supporters. This is especially true of Germany. Could this be due to the particularly good and beautiful large Continental dog breeds?

Strebel emphasizes that the Mastiff found scarcely any admirers in Germany and regretted it a great deal. The famous cynologist, Max Hartenstein from Plauen, was one of the few who imported two Mastiffs directly from England at the turn of the century. He paid the impressive price of 4200 gold marks for these animals. There is no evidence that this resulted in a separate breeding effort in Germany.

In *Die Kennzeichen unserer Rassehunde (The Characteristics of our Pedigree Dogs)*, by F. Bazille from the year 1926, the Mastiff is described under the rubric *Foreign breed, which appeared years ago at our shows only in natural breedings.* He includes a description of the breed, but no addresses of breeders and no club devoted to the breed is mentioned.

Mastiffs have only been supported systematically in Germany since 1968 under the auspices of the present Club for Molosser. This club has worked continuously for many years to bring German breeders into contact with breeding developments in other countries. From an international point of view, there is still a long way to go.

To give the reader an idea of the popularity of the Mastiff and the activities of the specialist clubs dedicated to them, here follows the national registration numbers in several countries at the club shows in 1982:

United States, 140 Mastiffs; Britain, 101 Mastiffs; the Netherlands, 42 Mastiffs; and Germany, 27 Mastiffs.

The newly arisen Mastiff is a breed that appeals to many dog fanciers. A well-built Mastiff is an imposing dog, a good watchdog, a dog with good character. Naturally, such a dog makes special demands in regard to feeding, care, and exercise. Optimally, it should be kept on a large property, which it would protect dependably.

Ch. Rodney Stone, the first 1000-pound Sterling Bulldog in the world, 1901.

English Bulldog. Photo by Isabelle Francais.

II. MODERN FIGHTING DOG BREEDS

Crufts champion in 1934, *Ch. Jasperdin of Din,* head study.

3. ENGLISH BULLDOG

It is known that time plays grim jokes on historical monuments. There has probably never been a dirtier joke, however, than the one played on our national symbol, the English Bulldog.

These critical words came from the pen of the dog expert, Rawdon B. Lee, and can be read in his book, *Modern Dogs,* from 1894. Lee adds that scholars had collected a wealth of historical material concerning the origin of this ancient breed of dog *but there is scarcely any convincing evidence that the dogs they report about have more than a passing similarity to the type of the Bulldog that was recognized in the year 1893.* This author arrives at the compelling conclusion, on the basis of the thorough comparison of old paintings and prints with the Bulldog of the year 1893, that the modern Bulldog is only a ghost of the old Bulldog described by historians.

Lee writes that good Bulldogs had still existed until about the year 1882, bred toward the old model, Rosa: *The lunacy of breeding for extreme exaggeration, for extreme foreheads and huge skulls, for totally exaggerated low-slung front legs, for shoulders pointing outward at almost a right angle, for Bulldogs with a front wider than that of the opposing bull. None of this used to be the case and only recently came into fashion.*

B. Marley supports this criticism in 1907 in Sydney Turner's *Kennel Encyclopedia: There is a kind of frenzy in the breeding for the widest possible chest. It has become fashionable to breed a dog whose elbows are turned completely*

II. MODERN FIGHTING DOG BREEDS

The imposing power of the Bulldog, *Sirloin of Pugilist*, 1934.

outwards, so that the chest appears broader than it really is. This more than anything else ruins the motion of the Bulldog.

From the contemporary literature of that time, we can and will quote a wealth of criticisms. These show how the stupidity of breeders, and lack of knowledge of the anatomical relationships of the Bulldog, repeatedly led to new faulty developments. The breeders truly played a dirty trick on this beautiful old dog breed!

We know that in the old days of bull baiting, breeders promoted anatomical anomalies. Then, after these cruelties were abolished, these anomalies were raised to the ideal of breeding. The breeders totally overlooked that this dog no longer had to creep on its belly toward the bull, that this creeping over the ground is a completely unnatural manner of locomotion. There was no longer a deadly horn over the Bulldog's back. Nonetheless, the wheel-like arched back of the Bulldog continued to be required. Although the dog no longer had to grip a bull's nose, it became all the more important to the breeders to perfect the severely upturned lower jaw, despite the fact that it was completely useless for a normal dog's life. The deeply set-back nose once brought the dog more fresh air as it gripped the bull. Now breeders further refined and perfected this nose, until the poor fellow was scarcely able to take in enough air through the extremely short nose. This seriously endangered the dog at high temperatures or when it was excited.

Instead of returning to a sound anatomical foundation after this dog was freed from its old bloody trade, breeders instead continued to "finish" the now totally superfluous perfect Bull Biter. The dog was forced to live with a ruined anatomy that was completely useless for daily life. As a result of exaggerations in breeding, it became a caricature of a fighting dog.

Nowadays we no longer have to confirm the goals strived for in breeding by baiting the bull; in fact, these anatomical cripples were not even suitable for bull baiting anymore. Now there was all the more room for fashionable excesses, for "freedom in breeding!" So breeders now turned their attention to "perfecting the Bulldog's head." When we read the standard we get the impression that the desired folds and wrinkles are far more important than the correct build of the hindquarters!

Head study of Olde English Bulldogge bred by David Leavitt, 1982.

The highest prices for English pedigree dogs before World War I were paid for Bulldogs. In 1901, Ch. Rodney Stone was sold to a buyer in New York for the sensational price of 1000 pounds Sterling, an unbelievable amount of money in those days! Our photograph shows a stately stud dog, the leading one of its time, which left behind first-class offspring. In those years it represented a milestone in English breeding. Up to 1909 it was followed by two more male Bulldogs, each time for the same high price, which was not achieved by any other English dog breed.

Because of the wealth of detailed individual requirements in the standard and the numerous grotesque anatomical anomalies, as well as extreme problems

II. MODERN FIGHTING DOG BREEDS

in reproduction, birth, and rearing, it has proved to be extraordinarily difficult to breed this dog in conformance with the standard. But—as in the past—there was a lot of money in it, so that new breeders were attracted all the time. Moreover, it was not always the big kennels that produced the champions. The little man also had a real chance, although he usually kept his breeding bitch as a family companion. This at least made birth and rearing easier than with bitches kept in the big kennels. Even in those days female Bulldogs were miserable mothers. This meant that the mother and puppies had to be watched over constantly. In many cases the puppies had to be reared by hand, which proved to be extremely difficult. Breeders who succeeded in rearing half the puppies were considered to be blessed with luck. Unfortunately, the Bulldog has passed these bad maternal traits on to many other breeds.

Over the years, there have repeatedly been new trends for breeders,

Backcross from the United States, David Leavitt, 1982.

supposedly based on the quest for the perfect Bulldog, directed toward the task of the bull fight, which had long since existed only in the imagination. Out of fairness to the breed and its fanciers, I will not give a detailed history of the development of the Bulldog. We could use the wealth of available photographs to show how many mazes breeders have stumbled through for nearly a century. A real horror show of sick, deformed animals!

Pickwick Nicco, bred by I. Angehrn, Switzerland, 1982.

I know that many Bulldog fanciers take a very strong personal interest in leading this old breed out of this maze. They need and deserve all the support we can give them. You do not violate a "sacred national object" and go unpunished! First I would like to present several really attractive photographs of the history of the breed. These are dogs that could be called beautiful in their own peculiar fashion, or at least very interesting and imposing.

The accounts available to me agree that the Bulldog reached its greatest popularity in the 1920s. Individual championship shows in England frequently registered more than 200 Bulldogs. Several photographs from the 1930s are worth a closer examination. A head study of the Crufts winner in 1934, Ch. Jasperdin of Din, probably exhibits the ideal head type of this breed. The photograph of Sirloin of Pugilist symbolizes the concentrated power of a male Bulldog of the time. The sire of Ch. Pugilist won a total of 30 C.C.s in his show career and was the leading stud dog in the period around 1930. Sirloin's son brought his breeder, Mrs. B. J. Walz, a handsome sum of money when he was exported to the United States. This male dog is distinguished by a first-class head, superb stance, substance, strong bones, and a back in conformance with the standard.

To understand what attracts people to this breed time and again, we cannot stop with the outward appearance, although this is often very impressive. For the Bulldog fan, however, the greatest attraction is the breed's lovable character.

The transformation of a dog full of ferocity and unbridled aggressiveness into a pleasant house dog by building up the highest possible stimulus threshold is the true achievement of the Bulldog breeder, which deserves full recognition. This is a self-confident, rather independent dog, free of any obsequiousness. It is a loving house dog that demands to be petted. It is an ideal nursemaid, not a yapper, and not always on the move. These are the true "sterling qualities" this dog offers us. I believe that the Bulldog's nature qualifies the breed as a house and family dog, particularly in the twentieth century!

The Bulldog has attracted numerous followers not only in the Anglo Saxon countries, but in Europe as well, where it found interest and support very early on. As early as 1897, Count Bylandt—by the way, himself an enthusiastic Bulldog fancier—in *Races de Chiens*

Pickwick Unique, Swiss Bulldog bitch, 1982.

Bulldog. Photo by Isabelle Francais.

reports of two Bulldog clubs in Germany, one in Stuttgart, the other in Berlin. In 1901 Cologne was added, and Düsseldorf in 1902. Additional clubs were founded in other cities and states. The German Bulldog fanciers were just as self-willed as their dogs, so that it took many years before all the clubs united in the Kontinental Bulldog-Klub in 1912.

It is easy to understand that this dog, as the English national symbol, had a hard time becoming established in Germany because of two murderous world wars. Fortunately, in today's unified Europe, such national prejudices are dying out.

Nonetheless, it is not uninteresting to read today the discussion of the breed by Professor Otto Fehringer from his book, *Unser Hund (Our Dog)*, which was published in 1940. If there is a note of nationalism here, we must concede that the breeding goals of the Bulldog made it easy for its critics to make reasonable objections.

Fehringer writes: *It really is beautiful in its ugliness and is permitted to have every imaginable fault, which would be rejected in any other dog. It epitomizes all the faults a dog could possibly have. The massive, much too powerful head is square, the skin hangs from it in folds, the lower jaw extends far in front of the upper jaw and is upward curving, often so strongly that this whole part of the muzzle looks as if squashed by a strong kick. Also, the lower front teeth are often unattractively exposed, the eyes are watery and protruding, and drooping flews round out this 'beautiful' dog's head. The massive body tapers peculiarly to the rear, so that it looks pear shaped. The clumsy hind legs stand higher than the front legs, which are set wide apart. Thus, the topline of the back cannot be straight and is called a 'roach back.' This curious build results in a peculiar, rolling gait. The tail is rather thick at the base and very quickly tapers to a fine point.*

This barely medium-sized, low-slung animal is truly a caricature of everything that a dog should be! As long as it is not blind, deaf, and one-eared, it has a chance to win in the show ring; otherwise, virtually anything is permitted.

I have intentionally quoted Professor Fehringer at length, because he shows the initial effect the Bulldog has on outsiders who know nothing about the history of the breed, and who have absolutely no interest in knowing what considerations went into the standard of the breed. He measures the anatomy with the same yardstick—and the Bulldog's build meets with no approval at all.

Let us not leave the German professor in a lurch, however, exposed to the silent wrath of all Bulldog fans. In *The Encyclopedia of Dogs* from the year 1970, which is supported by leading cynological clubs throughout the world, under the description of the Bulldog we find: *It is the result of a long process of selection, at the end of which stands a breed whose principal traits consist of pronounced anomalies!* This is not exactly flattery either!

Now, however, let us come to the defense of the Bulldog! It really cannot help it that the opponents of the breeding of pedigree dogs usually hold the Bulldog up as an example of how, through absurd excesses, man has turned sound, viable animals into caricatures and sick creatures. It is the victim, which makes it all the more surprising that, inside this hardly attractive shell, such a wonderful kernel lies hidden—the unique character of this animal. Let us recall again the print of Rosa and the pictures of the Duke of Hamilton's fighting Bulldogs. These should give us pause to consider the

II. MODERN FIGHTING DOG BREEDS

question of whether man has the right to "unlimited freedom in breeding!"

I think that the F.C.I. (Féderation Cynologique Internationale), as the leading European organization for the study of the dog, is moving in the right direction by having its scientific commission examine the standard of every breed to determine which standard regulations lead to unhealthy breeding. The consequence of this is that we breeders must breed viable pedigree dogs for the dog fancier and not permanent patients for the veterinarian!

It is a sign of the incompetence of the breed clubs that such considerations must be forced on them from the outside. Why do they still obstinately choose to hunt after phantoms, to cultivate fancies, to breed dogs suitable for bull baiting in our present world? The Bulldog was misbred for the sake of the grotesque, not to become the optimal opponent of the bull. And why is this dog not given a form appropriate to its present-day functions? Only because this dog comes from England, England has the national standard, and this is how things have been done for the last hundred years. And, for this reason, new ideas should be forbidden?

Aldridge Adele, German-bred Bulldog, 1982.

From the United States I received documents concerning an attempt to breed back to the original English Bulldog. Mr. David Leavitt had worked out his own breeding program, which would take a separate chapter to explain. He takes a mixture of one-half Bulldog, one-sixth American Pit Bull Terrier, one-sixth American Bulldog, and one-sixth Bullmastiff. From this combination he intends to create the old English Bulldog from the beginning of the nineteenth century. Our figures show the first results of this breeding in head study and frontal view. The dogs, according to Mr. Leavitt's theories, are supposed to be slightly larger and heavier than the modern Bulldog. It will probably take years before we can accurately judge the outcome of this experiment (a new breed of dog?). I believe, however, that the crossing in of such doubtful breeds as the Pit Bull Terrier and American Bulldog will only create additional, extraordinarily serious problems. [EDITOR'S NOTE: This "new" breed is called the Olde English Bulldogge and has been met with fair success.]

Below is a quote from the well-known Swiss Bulldog breeder, Imelda Angehrn, who wrote to me in 1982: *I am amazed by how often you take the words out of my mouth, for so much also applies to our breed. I have spent many years trying to establish soundness in the Bulldog. If you study the standard closely, many things that are always tolerated, and even desired out of ignorance, simply should not be. I think of loose shoulders, too-short neck, excessively undershot bite, large paws, steep hindquarters, corkscrew tail. . . and so forth. Too many and too thick wrinkles are also a serious fault. If we leave out these excesses, then we are not too far from your Bull Terrier, with the exception of the head and temperament, of course . . . It is a fundamental error to think that a Bulldog should not or must not be able to move . . .*"

Mrs. Angehrn has bred a number of beautiful Bulldogs, as shown by Pickwick Nicco and Pickwick Unique.

Now a few more remarks from this breeder, quoted from *Swiss Dog Sport*, July 16, 1982: *"The standard stipulates fine, thin wrinkles. Such Bulldogs also scarcely have problems with this. Unfortunately, however, at dog shows we often find dogs with too pronounced wrinkled heads and thick, fleshy folds, which readily become enflamed and then can lead to entropion of the eyelids. The public, of course, likes these 'crumpled creatures' the best. A great deal that would be to the good of the breed is in the hands of our judges . . . They should also have the courage to mark down a dog that under normal climatic conditions stands gasping, nearly suffocating, in the ring . . . A sound, good Bulldog must be able to move lightly and nimbly. It is a shame that there are judges who scarcely allow our dogs to run in the course of judging.*

I am convinced that many points could be improved without giving the Bulldog a substantially different appearance. The front and head must become somewhat less massive and broad again. When nice, broad, well-rounded cheeks are present, you could also get used to a bit more nose, providing that this actually made breathing easier. For good movement and easier births, a slightly longer topline should be tolerated, as well as a broader pelvis.

With many breeds, the standard itself is less lacking than the way in which it is implemented or interpreted. Many excesses are simply accepted, although they do not have to be and are not written down anywhere."

Mrs. Imelda Angehrn is much more familiar than I with the problems of the Bulldog; after all, she has bred more

II. MODERN FIGHTING DOG BREEDS

than 90 litters of English Bulldogs. For this reason I have quoted her at length. I believe that her reasonable approach and her opposition to exaggerated interpretations of the standard make sense and would be useful throughout the world.

Anyone who comes to know and love the Bulldog, with its charmingly grim and tender character, sees in this breed of dog an innocent victim of foolish breeding by humans for centuries. He simply cannot help but wish to make this breed anatomically sound as soon as possible. It is high time for an open discussion of how we can give the Bulldog a functional anatomy again. The Bulldog bitch Rosa was the right choice as the goal of breeders throughout the nineteenth century. But what way leads back to Rosa?

Mrs. Angehrn wrote me about my Bull Terrier books: *When I look at your many wonderful photographs in the books, I could turn green with envy: What would this mean for the wonderful Bulldog, maybe a trace softer in the lines, a bit more deeply and broadly hung—and with 'my' heads on top. It would be the realization of a great dream, were I ever to approach this!*

The Bull Terrier as the savior of the old English Bulldog? Surely it could give this breed something of the anatomical harmony achieved in the last thirty years! And it would be service in return for all the good gifts the Bulldog gave the Bull Terrier in 1860! A risky thought, a fancy—which flies in the face of all modern rules of pedigree-dog breeding!

Chien de Nuit (Keeper's Night Dog), France, 1890.

Mr. Leavitt also thought about this, and then acted. Will success continue? Mrs. Angehrn also thought about it. I have to say that I find her vision to be most realistic.

4. BULLMASTIFF

Buffon describes in 1791 that crossing the Mastiff with the Bulldog produced very interesting and useful half-breds. This was hardly realized by to the English gamekeepers at the turn of the twentieth century when they crossed these two old breeds to produce the ideal dog for their profession. On the great estates of England, poaching was becoming more and more of a threat at this time. Because of the harsh penalties the poachers faced if caught, they preferred to shoot it out with the gamekeepers than surrender.

What was needed was a large, fast dog of muted color. It should be able to knock down the poachers silently in the night with a mighty charge. Then it was supposed to hold down the poacher until the gamekeeper could disarm and arrest him. Numerous breeding attempts were made, and the best dogs were clearly produced by crossing the Mastiff and Bulldog. What argued against the direct use of these breeds to protect the gamekeepers was that at the turn of the century the Bulldog was already too small, was too disobedient, and stubbornly sank its teeth in its opponent after it attacked. On the other hand, the Mastiff was too large, not fast enough, and it lacked the will to attack without prior warning.

The result of crossing the two breeds was a large-framed, fearless, and temperamental dog that fought silently. It attacked the poacher silently without warning from the cloak of darkness, knocked him to the ground with the force of the charge, and held him dependably without mauling him. Truly imposing protection for the beleaguered gamekeeper!

Farcraft Fidelity, the key male in the breeding of the Bullmastiff, 1923.

It is very interesting that in many European countries at the same time and for similar reasons large guard dogs of this kind were bred for gamekeepers. These dogs even had logically consistent names in the individual countries.

The English dog was known at first as the Gamekeeper's Night Dog. The dog was mentioned by this name starting in 1867 in English books and magazines. In France we find the *Chien de Nuit,* the night dog, and a picture of this former French breed was taken from *Les Chiens D'Arre't* by Caillard 1890. The spiked collar protected the dog from being held by its own collar.

Now let us return to Britain, to the Gamekeeper's Night Dog. The famous Count Vivian Hollender called for the recognition of the Bullmastiff as a separate dog breed in March 1911 in the magazine *The Kennel*. He says that the old English Bulldog has given Britain two wonderful new breeds of dog, the

II. MODERN FIGHTING DOG BREEDS

white Bull Terrier, which Count Hollender was intimately associated with his whole life, and recently the Bullmastiff, whose recognition Count Hollender campaigned for. In the last 30 years the Bullmastiff has not only proved its wonderful ability as a companion dog of the gamekeeper, now police stations are becoming increasingly interested in this dependable guard dog. In contrast to the Airedale Terrier frequently used by the police, the Bullmastiff is big and strong enough even to quickly overpower armed criminals. Hollender emphasizes the special teachability of this dog in its training as a police dog.

Count Hollender illustrates his speech in defense of the Bullmastiff with an early photograph of the famous Thorneywood Terror. Our reproduction of this picture suffers from the poor quality of the original photograph, but it is the earliest pictorial document of the history of the Bullmastiff breed. Terror and his breeder, Mr. W. Burton, were the successful pioneers for the recognition of the crossbred as an independent dog breed.

As early as the show held from September 2 to 9, 1871 in the Crystal Palace in London, six Yard or Keeper's Night Dogs of very different outward appearance were shown. The first real sensation, however, was caused by Mr. Burton's Thorneywood Terror at his appearance at a number of dog shows in 1900 and 1901. The magazine *The Field* reported that at such dog shows Mr. Burton offered one pound to any man who could escape from Terror while securely muzzled. One of the spectators who had experience with dogs volunteered and amused a large assembly of sportsmen and keepers who had gathered there.

The man was given a long start and

Thorneywood Terror, Bullmastiff, 1900.

the muzzled dog slipped after him. The animal caught him immediately and knocked down this man with the first spring. The latter bravely tried to hold his own, but was floored every time he got to his feet, ultimately being kept to the ground until the owner of the dog released him. The man had three rounds with the powerful canine, but was

Ostmaston Turk, Bullmastiff, 1910.

Bullmastiff. Photo by Isabelle Francais.

beaten each time and was unable to escape.

At the turn of the century, this male dog was considered to be one of the most intelligent and best-trained dogs in the whole country. The dog was so famous that a separate demonstration was arranged for a representative of the War Ministry.

A second pioneer and experienced breeder of this new breed was Mr. Biggs with his Ostmaston Bullmastiff. What was previously said applies to the male dog Ostmaston Turk as well. This 54-kilogram male dog descended from a dam that was the product of a cross between a Mastiff and a Bloodhound. In these years it is certain that other breeds of dog were also crossed in, among others the Great Dane. It is astounding how Turk already represents the new breed in build and head type.

It is interesting that this dog breed suffered far less during World War I than did its big ancestor, the Mastiff. Mr. S. E. Moseley founded the Farcroft kennel immediately after the war. This breeder became the leading personality,

Modern Bullmastiff.

II. MODERN FIGHTING DOG BREEDS

the father of the Bullmastiff, comparable to a James Hinks, the creator of the white Bull Terrier, or a Rittmeister von Stephanitz, who played a decisive role in shaping the modern German Shepherd Dog. We are indebted to S. E. Moseley from Burslem for breeding the Bullmastiff.

Farcraft Fidelity, whelped on September 4, 1921, bred by S. E. Moseley, became the cornerstone for breeding the Bullmastiff. In 1926, at five years of age, it was the best male Bullmastiff at the Crufts dog show. This was the big debut of the new dog breed following its recognition by the English Kennel Club. It is thanks to this male dog that Farcraft Kennel brought about 80 percent of all prizes at the shows back to Burslem from 1925 to 1927. Fidelity was never defeated by any rival, including its own offspring, during its show career.

Mr. Moseley based the great success of his kennel on direct crosses between the Mastiff and the Bulldog. These crosses were carried out to obtain a ratio of 6:4 Mastiff to Bulldog. He then started a systematic line breeding with these dogs. His main goal, besides the good temperament of his dogs, was an absolutely correct anatomical build. He preferred a somewhat smaller dog with a shoulder height of 66 centimeters over larger dogs with shoulder heights up to 76 centimeters. These dogs, as a rule, owed their shoulder height to the crosses with the Great Dane. Moseley was uncompromising in demanding an active, substantial, and mobile dog. He rejected the cow-hocked rears and splayed feet that often turned up. His goal in breeding was: *Big enough to have a lot of strength, but not too big to lose mobility and activity! Faithful and fearless, but never vicious!*

At a shoulder height of 71

Lasso vom Antoniushof.

centimeters, Farcraft Fidelity weighed 53 kilograms. In 1925, 16 bitches and 5 stud dogs stood at Farcraft Kennel, and about a hundred puppies were whelped a year. Mr. Moseley was considered to be an excellent businessman, and soon managed to place his dogs with prominent Englishmen. He also systematically built up an export trade in Bullmastiffs during this time. Farcraft Bullmastiffs went all over the world, including the United States, Africa, Canada, France, the Netherlands, Belgium, Germany, and Italy, to name only a few places.

As a kind of Christmas present, the Kennel Club opened a separate show class for the new breed at recognized dog shows on Christmas Day 1924. The announcement clearly restricted entry to Bullmastiffs that had been bred purely as Bullmastiffs for at least three generations without the crossing in of the original breeds. In October 1927 there followed the final recognition of the new breed when it was registered in the breed register of the Kennel Club as a new English dog breed. These rapid advances could be traced back to the activities of The National Bull-mastiff Police-Dog Club, which was founded in 1925 and whose first president was Mr. S. E. Moseley. Interesting and for Britain very unusual was the linking of the name of the pedigree dog club with the function of the new breed as a police dog. This, too, was part of the successful advertising campaign by Mr. Moseley on behalf of the Bullmastiff.

The breed developed quite favorably in the 1930s. More than 700 puppies were registered in the stud book in 1938. Prior to 1930 the annual number of puppies was under 200. Naturally, World War II also posed a serious threat to this large dog breed with its corresponding big appetite. In 1941 the number of registrations fell to 80 puppies. It is all the more surprising that the breeders also mastered these problems and wisely kept their best breeding stock in the country. At the first post-war shows in late 1945 and in May 1946, the Bullmastiffs returned to competition with very balanced breeding stock. It created quite a stir that the Bullmastiff was represented by 64 entries of excellent quality at the first post-war Crufts dog show in October 1948. Thanks to the sacrifices of its breeders and fanciers, the Bullmastiff breed got through this catastrophic time very well. What a contrast to the sad picture of the post-war woes experienced by the English Mastiff breeders!

Let me conclude with a few comments about the standard of the breed. Of particular importance here is the general description of the breed. According to the standard, the Bullmastiff is a very powerfully built, symmetrical dog. It has great strength, without appearing heavy. Its nature combines great intelligence, reliability, and activity, paired with stamina and alertness. In dogs a shoulder height of approximately 63.5 to 68.5 centimeters and a weight of 45 to 59 kilograms is expected. Bitches should be 61 to 66 centimeters at the shoulder and weigh 41 to 50 kilograms. A clear requirement is that size and weight must always be in proper proportion. An anatomically sound build and mobility are fundamental traits of a good Bullmastiff.

Following the reports of the numerous exaggerations in breeding practiced with the Mastiff and Bulldog, it is a pleasure to present the positive development of the Bullmastiff in Britain. For me the Bullmastiff is the soundest representative of the large breeds of fighting dog. Here the function of the dog was viewed correctly over the decades. The standard is not directed by the vision of old fighting competitions, but by the usable dog. Mr. Moseley also recognized early on that largeness and heaviness can be more detrimental than beneficial to a dog. The beauty of the Bullmastiff is not only proof of the good anatomy of the breed but it also reveals something about the reliable nature of the dog.

It is a shame that this beautiful and good English dog breed has attracted so few admirers in Germany so far, although we previously reported on very early imports from the Farcraft kennel. The Molosser Club has regulated the breed since 1969. In 1982, for example, only three litters with a total of 13 puppies were produced in all of Germany. At important shows we find—in the best of circumstances—about five animals in the ring. A representative of the Bullmastiff in Germany is Lasso vom Antoniushof.

Happily we can report that the Bullmastiff enjoys great popularity in the Scandinavian countries, in Sweden, Norway, and Finland. In Finland there were 280 Bullmastiffs in the early 1980s, and a substantial number is bred there every year. It is the hope of the fanciers of beautiful and good large dogs, that the Bullmastiff will soon attract many new fanciers in Germany. It certainly deserves to have them.

5. BORDEAUX DOG

Gaston Phoebus described large-framed molossoid dogs as early as the fourteenth century in France. We are thus justified in assuming that these were the ancestors of the large-framed fighting dogs that were kept throughout the Mediterranean region along the coasts of Spain, France, and Italy. In the nineteenth century, these countries had similar social conditions as in the "Black Country" of Britain. Animal fights were the big attraction for the oppressed populace. The fights between bears, wolves, leopards, or wild asses and large fighting dogs were an outlet for the people to work off their aggression. Dog versus dog fights were also widespread.

In southern France we find the center of these fights in the region around Bordeaux. This city gave its name to the

Bordeaux Dog. Photo by Isabelle Francais.

Bordeaux Dog, *Sultane*, from a print in the "Journal Chasse et Pêche," 1892.

large fighting dogs bred in this coastal region, thereby creating the Bordeaux Dog.

Graf Bylandt, in the French edition of his book in 1897, includes the portrait of the bitch Sultane. The engraving gives a good impression of the raw power and strength of this early Bordeaux Dog. Bylandt sees in the breed a fortunate union of the high qualities of the Mastiff and Bulldog. We must not, however, misunderstand this interpretation. Bordeaux is not the cradle of the brother of the English Bullmastiff. In the origin of the Bordeaux Dog, the large native dogs

II. MODERN FIGHTING DOG BREEDS

encountered along the entire coast certainly make up the main part of the breeding material. There is no doubt that these dogs bred exclusively for animal fights were then crossed with the large-framed Spanish Bulldog and the Mastiff to improve the native breed.

A uniform breed type of the Bordeaux Dog did not exist before about 1920. It is interesting to compare the illustrations selected by Bylandt in 1897. Had the dogs not been presented under the title Dogue de Bordeaux, we would scarcely have classified them in the same breed. Here follows a remark by Professor J. Kunstler from Bordeaux, who wrote in 1914: *"je ne connais pas deux chiens en Bordeaux, qui se resemblent* (I know of no two dogs in Bordeaux that are similar to each other)." And Professor Kunstler was considered at that time to be one of the leading experts in the breeding of the Bordeaux Dog.

Robert Leighton reports in his *Book of the Dog* in 1907 that the Bordeaux Dog initially attracted great interest from several English Bulldog breeders, and that after 1880 good dogs were imported from France. The English supporters were impressed with this French breed. This French dog was ferocious and strong and had a powerful build. It was systematically made vicious and was given warm blood to drink to make it even more aggressive. The French placed emphasis on keeping the old breeding lines pure. Black masks were considered an indication of the crossing in of the Mastiff. As an important indication of the purity of the breed, attention was paid to the leather-colored nose, light eyes, and a red mask.

The old Bordeaux Dogs brought to Britain were highly prized in France. The buyers, however, apparently were particularly proud of the scar-covered dogs' bodies. They clearly came from injuries incurred in dog fights or in bear baiting. Thus, the British at this time apparently had not yet conquered the specter of the bloody sports of their past. In Leighton's opinion, the banning

Bordeaux Dog, circa 1930.

of ear cropping ruined the victorious advance of the Bordeaux Dog in Britain.

Bylandt's description of the breed in 1897 presents a dog of powerful, somewhat low-slung build, a massive, muscular, heavy dog with a particularly huge head. Anything that recalls the crossing in of the Mastiff is considered a fault. Bordeaux Dogs that were trained to fight were extremely dangerous opponents, but those kept as family dogs were of a gentle character.

In the year 1911 Professor J. Kunstler published his own standard of the breed, which, for the most part, was adopted. He urgently warned against the adulteration of the breed by unscrupulous breeders and dealers. In his standard, Bylandt's well-known call for substance and great strength was elevated to a requirement. The Bordeaux must be built like a cob, a powerful, low-slung coach horse. Kunstler considers the ideal shoulder height to be approximately 65 centimeters, and the correct weight to be approximately 45 to 55 kilograms. In 1897 Bylandt still found weights of 65 to 85 kilograms!

Alarming is the standard requirement introduced by Kunstler, according to which the circumference of the Bordeaux Dog's skull must equal its shoulder height. He proceeds from the assumption that no dog breed in the world could have a more massive skull! Thereby—as has previously been documented with other breeds—in total ignorance of anatomical and physical laws, the standard of the breed contains the basis for necessarily breeding for serious anatomical faults. This "most massive skull" had to seriously impede the dog's motion. In the standard of this breed we again find a wealth of extremely detailed requirements concerning the dog's head.

Of great interest is Kunstler's clear affirmation of the black mask. *The red mask, which has too little pigment, was once considered a specific trait, but*

Chanelle v. Storchennest, German-bred Bordeaux Dog.

II. MODERN FIGHTING DOG BREEDS 105

Head study of *Ch. Orgo de l'Étang des Aieux.*

completely unjustly. It is a sign of degeneration, which is based particularly on the too intensive use of similar blood. In other words, the stylized red mask is a clear indication of degeneration from inbreeding.

I have a particularly interesting photograph from the 1930s at hand, which, according to the caption, portrays a well-known French show winner. Even so, this animal weighed 63 kilograms and to me also was amazingly similar to the old Sultane. This photograph seems particularly significant to me, however, because for experts it represents an interesting link to the backcrossing with the Mastino Napoletano. Is it not also evidence for the common origin of these large dog breeds that originated in the Mediterranean region? The photograph also documents that at this time the Bordeaux Dog was often cropped, which absolutely was permitted by the standard.

As the only large foreign molossoid breed, the Bordeaux Dog became known in Germany after World War I. In 1924 a separate club was founded, the direct predecessor of the present-day Molosser Club. In 1926 the German Bordeaux Dog Club already had 65 members. The main centers of breeding were Thuringia and Saxony.

Here is the standard description of the Bordeaux Dog by F. Bazille in 1926: *In appearance like a terrible, sturdy, powerful, imposing athlete.* The most popular size was 63 to 66 centimeters at the shoulder, with a weight of 45 to 55 kilograms.

In the German Bordeaux Club, for a long time there were disagreements about the red and black masks—as if the breed did not have other problems! The red masks were justifiably criticized as a loss of color from many years of inbreeding, and were considered a measure of inbreeding degeneration. The supporters of the red masks in turn saw in these animals the only old French bloodline that had not been contaminated by the Mastiff. These supporters completely misunderstood that totally different physical characters other than this loss of color were available for judging the amount of Mastiff influence.

Although the Bordeaux Dogs were represented in the Deutscher Kartell für Hundewesen (DKH) as the only foreign molossoid breed, we must not overestimate the significance of the breed at this time. At dog shows in the 1930s about 10 to 20 Bordeaux Dogs were shown a year and five to eight litters were registered a year. The breed, therefore, had found a rather small circle of supporters.

Problems must not be passed over in silence. Experts rightly criticize the rather short life expectancy of the Bordeaux Dog. The gastric torsion (bloat) that affects large dog breeds, in particular, has plagued this breed. A pioneer for the breed in Germany, Werner Preugschat, writes: *A large number of our Bordeaux Dogs have died from this illness in their prime from three to six years of age.* But not only the susceptibility to this illness leads Werner Preugschat to observe that absolutely the only thing he would retain in the breed is its good temperament, but he has serious reservations about the disproportion of breeding for extreme heads to the detriment of the soundness of the breed and its natural motion. *What am I supposed to do with a dog that has a monstrous skull and is at most able to carry it from the food dish to its bed?* Harsh words, but he is right when he takes exception to breeding for huge heads and the lack of knowledge of the anatomical relationships that could ruin a breed. Unfortunately, I still have to present additional examples of this. The dog is a running predator, not a block of stone, which man can chisel away at as he sees fit. Unfortunately this a red flag, which we will find throughout this book.

Conditions did not exactly seem to be optimal for the survival of the Bordeaux Dog after World War II. The leading German breeders, even the active Bordeaux Dog breeder, Maria Pufahl, criticize the alarming shrinkage of the breeding stock, which repeatedly forces the use of further inbreeding. In the years 1970 to 1980, fewer than 20 puppies a year were bred in Germany. Moreover, Germany is one of the few countries, outside of the motherland of France, in which the breed has found a true home.

The United States and Britain, the great reservoir of the English fighting dog breeds, ignore this dog. Neither the Kennel Club of England, nor the American Kennel Club, recognize this breed. There are a few fanciers in the Netherlands, Switzerland, and Italy.

New initiatives will soon be required if the Bordeaux Dog can hope to flourish again in Germany. A few imports from France are being registered.

From France we receive the pronouncement of the President of the French Bordeaux Dog Club: "The Bordeaux Dog lives!" Now, if he stresses this, then there must have been serious doubt about the breed's survival before. The optimism is based on the good number of entries today at shows in France today. For example, 25 dogs entered the show in Paris, and 68 dogs entered the show in Bordeaux on July 4, 1982. Except for the motion, the quality of these dogs is supposed to have been quite good.

It is to be hoped that the few remaining survivors of this interesting old breed will be sufficient for its recovery.

6. FRENCH BULLDOG

For the enthusiastic Bulldog fancier, Berta Burkert from Munich, the French Bulldog is: *A 'wonder dog', who cheers the sad, brings the dreamy back to the present, and shows consideration to the lazy. In short—a house dog par excellence!*

We have learned to know and admire the Bulldog as the English national symbol. So how in the world is it possible that a completely separate Bulldog originated in France, which today competes successfully with the English Bulldog for supporters throughout the world.

We know of a serious economic crisis in old England in the years from 1848 to 1860, which had a particularly grave effect on the textile and clothing industries. The hopeless situation was the reason for the emigration of the English lace makers to Normandy in France and Belgium. The artisans were welcomed there with open arms and became the foundation of a new center of textile manufacturing. Many emigrants settled particularly in the region around Calais.

The new homeland, as a rule, offered only small apartments or very small houses, so that their inhabitants needed small dogs, which could adapt optimally to these cramped living conditions. Precisely in Nottingham, the place the workers emigrated from, the breeding of small Bulldogs flourished in the middle of the nineteenth century. What could be more sensible than to bring the smallest of these Bulldogs to France, since they could be expected to adapt optimally to the new conditions? Moreover, they were a tangible link to the old homeland!

The breeding of small Bulldogs still occurred throughout Britain at this time. At the first dog shows in the 1860s there often were more Bulldogs in the classes for small dogs than for large ones, and most of them weighed less than 10 kilograms. Their popularity then dropped off and it is reported that enterprising dealers from London and Birmingham (James Hinks!) used this opportunity to sell these small Bulldogs, which were now in less demand in Britain, for good prices to the emigrants.

In France the small Bulldogs proved to be quite useful and adaptable, and they soon went from Normandy to the large French cities, especially Paris with its many suburbs. The small Bulldog became the dog of the little man. It was no doubt frequently bred with the native dogs, because the Bulldog was considered to be a guarantee for a fearless temperament. These crossbreds were named Terrier-boule, and are the transitional form to the French Bulldog.

Around the year 1860, a loose association was founded of like-minded fanciers, all proud owners of their Terrier-boules. A. and E. Gay, the authors of the monograph of the breed that was published in 1871, described the members of the organization as a *collection of butchers, rag pickers, policemen, coffee-house owners, whitewashers, marble cutters, prostitutes, coachmen, and porters from the Parisian market halls.* And all of them loved their dogs! There were 47 founding members. Starting in 1885 they met weekly in the dog market, starting in 1886 in the bird market. They bred their little Terrier-boules and lived with others of their kind. There were small dealings between them, but no wealthy people who showed an interest in these dogs.

The club was called Club Amical, and in 1888 it drew up its own charter and a first standard of the breed. The goal of breeding was: "The dog looks like a small Hercules and should be equally tall as long." The maximum weight was 15 kilograms for male dogs and $12^{1}/_{2}$ kilograms for bitches. In 1896 this standard was supplemented by the unalterable requirement for the "bat ear," the "trademark of the new breed."

That the breeding of a square dog had not yet been achieved is shown by an early illustration of the bitch, Pierce, owned by M. J. Cotelle from Paris. We are indebted to Count Bylandt for this print. He writes in 1897 that several years earlier in France a new Bulldog had been bred, which differed from the English Bulldog in having a prick ear; the maximum size was 30 centimeters, the maximum weight under 10 kilograms.

When the French Bulldog came back to Britain through imports in 1893, there were massive protests and a nationalistic outcry. Lady Kathleen Pilkinton wrote: *This is nothing else but the rebirth of a breed. The lace makers from Nottingham of course already knew of the Toy Bulldog in 1840. We cannot say that it developed into something better during its stay in France. In 1893 it returned with a perfect French accent, with excellent manners, but with loathsome bat ears and an unattractive undershot jaw.* Not a particularly warm greeting for the "lost son!"

Was it true that nothing else had changed with the crossbred form of the Terrier-boule? The first thing that catches the eye is the reference to the "excellent manners." Thus, apparently the extreme aggressiveness of the English ancestors had been bred out of the dogs in France, which was certainly absolutely necessary for the cramped conditions in the homes.

French Bulldog. Photo by Isabelle Francais.

By chance there are two valuable Bulldog bronzes in my collection, one from England portraying the Toy Bulldog, the other a Viennese bronze showing the French Bulldog, which enjoyed great popularity in this city. Both bronzes date from the late nineteenth century. With such true-to-nature models, differences are easy to comment on.

First we can determine that in the breeding of the English Bulldog, prick ears occurred in the Toy Bulldog and were not forbidden by the standard until 1907. For this reason we find prick ears in both the English and French model. The difference in ear carriage is important. In the English model it is laterally to the outside, in the French model it is positioned directly to the front. The stop is not well defined in the English model but is clearly accented in the French. The forehead groove divides the head vertically in the English Bulldog, but in the French Bulldog the forehead is rounded and the forehead groove has disappeared completely; the paws are broad in the English Bulldog with a soft anterior metatarsus but are bony with firm hocks in the French Bulldog. I believe that a comparison of these bronzes shows quite clearly the difference between the two breeds at the turn of the century.

French Bulldog bitch, *Pierce*, circa 1895.

II. MODERN FIGHTING DOG BREEDS

In 1898 the French Bulldog is recognized as a new French breed by the leading French dog organization, the Société Canine. The characteristic bat ears are the differentiating character to the English Toy Bulldog, in which rose ears are required. The Toy Bulldog experiences another renaissance because of the active competition from France, which ends, however, with World War I. By means of a series of international agreements, the French standard is recognized throughout the world, although it must be emphasized that the difference between the French and the English Bulldog goes much, much further than the different ear shapes. A glance at these early illustrations document that the French Bulldog is related to the English Bulldog, but is in no way—as the Toy Bulldog—a true-to-scale diminution of the English Bulldog. The victory march of this new dog from Paris goes as a kind of Parisian fashion through the dog world. Particularly in the large cities, such as Berlin, Vienna, London, Brussels, and New York, the breed finds numerous enthusiastic supporters. The head with the unique

English Bulldog bronze, *Toy Bulldog,* circa 1890 (Dr. Fleig's collection).

Viennese bronze, French Bulldog, circa 1890 (Dr. Fleig's collection).

bat ears fascinates women in particular, and it becomes the companion dog of the lady of the world.

Germany can legitimately be counted among the leading breeding nations and has continually supported this distinctive dog breed. In the year 1870, Max Hartenstein was one of the German occupiers of Paris. There he became acquainted with and prized the Terrier-boule and ten years later brought the French Bulldog back to Berlin. Strebel writes that Hartenstein had in fact brought back the best of all from Paris, at prices that ran into the thousands for good specimens. These high prices were justified in that the low number of puppies, birthing difficulties, and susceptibility of the puppies to disease made breeding extremely difficult. We present these early imports by Hartenstein, Loubet and Myrot, in an illustration by Strebel, which demonstrates the high standard of these imports, in comparison, for example, to the old Pierce. We should also mention that in 1913 the bitch Patrice Plavia,

This way up! Grimmelsburg Bulldog.

II. MODERN FIGHTING DOG BREEDS

Ape or French Bulldog?

Imports from France, from Strebel, circa 1900.

from the Hartenstein's kennel in Berlin, was judged the "most beautiful French Bulldog on the Continent" in Paris over 120 rivals.

The German Breeding Club for the French Bulldog was founded in 1909 in Munich, the second center of German breeding. By 1926 the German stud book contained 5500 registrations from 60 kennels and 500 members. The popularity of the breed continued to increase until the year 1939.

After World War II, the German breeding stocks were systematically rebuilt through the first importations from the Netherlands, Switzerland, Britain, and France. One kennel in particular linked up to Max Hartenstein's great success: S. D. Prince Alexander von Ratibor and Corvey at Unterriexingen Castle. His French Bulldogs enjoy a great international reputation.

It would be beyond the scope of this book to describe individually the successes of the French Bulldog in France, Britain, the United States, the Netherlands, Austria, and Switzerland. Did you know that Mrs. Sacher, in the Sacher Hotel in Vienna, was always accompanied by her French Bulldog when she greeted the guests? Or how many artists, actors, or singers chose

Typical German-bred male (v. Ratibor and Corvey), 1980.

French Bulldogs at Unterriexingen Castle, 1980.

II. MODERN FIGHTING DOG BREEDS

this small dog as their life's companion?

Now let me make a somewhat critical observation. The little Frenchman has also remained a Bulldog, but after its move to France was able to avoid the extreme exaggerations we found in the breeding of its English relatives. We have previously mentioned the difficulties in its breeding, but you can easily accept these faults. Obviously, the standard requirement for an extremely short nose for this dog does not exactly make breathing or running easier. The little "muscle-man" carries a lot of weight in proportion to its body size and the desired roach back does not help its motion. All in all, it can be said of this breed, in comparison to certain others, that it has largely remained free of exaggerations by breeders.

I demonstrate this with special pleasure by means of two very charming "climbing Bulldogs from the Grimmelsburg". For the photographs I am indebted to their breeders, the Dr. Grimm family in Bad Reichenhall.

In closing, allow me to say one more thing about this dog breed. I don't know of more ideal dog for keeping in the city apartment, no better playmate for the children. My wife hopes that such a French Bulldog will be our family companion in our old age.

The dog is a little, big-headed monster that needs and gives love—you could fall in love with this Bulldog!

7. BULL TERRIER

In the skillful hands of James Hinks in Birmingham in the 1860s, the Bull and Terrier was transformed into a new pedigree dog, the snow-white Bull Terrier. His son, James Hinks II, describes this transformation: *The cross was ideal, for it united the strength of the Bulldog with the speed and intelligence of the terrier. The big change came about toward the end of the 1850s. My father owned dogs from the bravest of the old breeds and had experimented in their breeding. He had also crossed in the white English Terrier and the Dalmation. In this way he produced a pure-white dog, which he named the Bull Terrier. These dogs were much improved in appearance. The Bulldog's appearance was largely bred out, the dogs were longer and more elongated in the head, more robust in the muzzle, free of flews and loose skin on the throat. The necks were more highly arched, and in temperament the animals were more intelligent and livelier.*

After a short time they became the embodiment of the old fighting dog, but more civilized. All the rough edges had been smoothed off, without making the dogs too gentle. Fast, active, courageous, muscular—and simultaneously a real gentleman. Naturally, this change brought the Bull Terrier many admirers, and the milk-white dog was sought after everywhere."

With the English and French Bulldogs, we previously encountered James Hinks, an uncommonly clever businessman. He was doubtlessly one of old England's most significant breeder personalities. Within a few years he won success with his pure-white dogs at shows throughout Britain. The new color and the elegant form made the Bull Terrier presentable. The old bloody business of the dog fights still hung over the old Bull and Terrier; it was stamped as the companion to shady characters. It continued to remain in the lower classes of the population, while the wide world of a flourishing pedigree-dog breeding stood open to its white brother.

James Hinks also demonstrated to the public the elegance and first-class anatomy of the Bull Terrier, as well as to those who doubted its capabilities. In one of the illegal dog fights, Hink's

Bull Terrier. Photo by Isabelle Francais.

white bitch, Puss, proved that these white dogs had retained the genuine fighting dog qualities by easily beating the much larger and heavier opponent of the old breed.

The breed had its first heyday in the years 1868 to 1895, when it was "in" to have such an elegant, brave white dog. The dog was admired greatly, particularly by young people. The Bull Terrier Club, one of the best-run dog breeding clubs in the world, was founded in 1887. The standard of the breed adopted in the same year established the requirement for a first-class anatomical build—without exaggerations—combined with the retention of the typical temperament and the pure-white color. This breed standard was adopted throughout the world, although in subsequent years in the most diverse countries attempts were made here and there to introduce some variation into the breed. Nonetheless, over the years, the motherland of the breed proved to be absolutely autonomous and sovereign in the determination of the standard and the breeding goals.

The breed suffered a very serious setback from the ban against cropping issued by The Kennel Club in 1895, which banned all cropped dogs without exception from English dog shows. Heavy drop ears, as well as flapping prick ears, disfigured badly the sharply chiseled skull of the Bull Terrier, and the breed lost many of its supporters and breeders.

An example of the high standing of the breed is the large-framed Bloomsburry King, whelped on July 10, 1898. This dog was banned from all dog shows because its breeder, H. E. Monk, had it cropped in the old style after an accident injured the ears. Nonetheless, the male dog was universally recognized for its excellence and was used extensively for breeding. Its first-class offspring confirmed its value. King also has a wonderfully sound anatomical build, even by modern standards.

Bloomsburry King, one of the best stud dogs of its time, print by R. H. Moore, 1898.

To demonstrate the quality of this powerful Bull Terrier at the turn of the century, we can consider an illustration of a Bull Terrier hunting rats. The famous painter, Maud Earl, has captured this scene in her watercolor, "A Morning Nip".

Within about twenty years, the English breeders had succeeded in changing the formerly cropped ears into a stiff prick ear, which again suited the head form. Allowing Bull Terriers to go out into the world with drop ears was inconceivable to them. In this way these breeders proved that you could transform drop ears into prick ears not only with the cropping knife, but through systematic breeding as well, if this necessitated by the head form of a dog breed. Will this example by taken up by other breeds with similar problems today?

After the lowest point at the start of the century, the annual number of registrations of the Bull Terrier with The Kennel Club averaged about 300 dogs a year up to World War I. In 1918, however, the number dropped to 61, a precipitous drop in the number bred. The breed soon recovered, however, and by the middle of the twentieth century about 1000 puppies were bred a year.

The basic requirement of Bull Terrier breeding established by Hinks, to preserve the dog's particularly good character—full of fire, but of a friendly temperament and ready to obey—runs through the breed to the present. We can say without arrogance that this goal was largely achieved. This is no doubt that this is the explanation for the ever growing popularity of the Bull Terrier.

Of course there were also excesses by breeders with these dogs. The white color became a kind of creed for its supporters. Breeders and judges, who, beginning in about 1920, tried to breed colored Bull Terriers and to place them at shows, had a very hard time of it and virtually had to tilt at windmills. Miss Montague Johnstone, after a decade of systematic breeding, with her Romany kennel achieved the big breakthrough with her colored Bull Terrier. We are indebted to her for the total equality of the colored and white Bull Terrier today.

When white Bull Terriers from colored ancestors were to be crossed into the pure-white lines preserved since Hinks's time, this came within a hair's breadth of creating a schism in the venerable Bull Terrier Club. To breed descendants of colored ancestors with the noble white lines was considered to be little less than scandalous in the breed. For all that, these colored dogs saved the breed from a great danger:

Head study of *Yogi Alemannentrutz*, 1982.

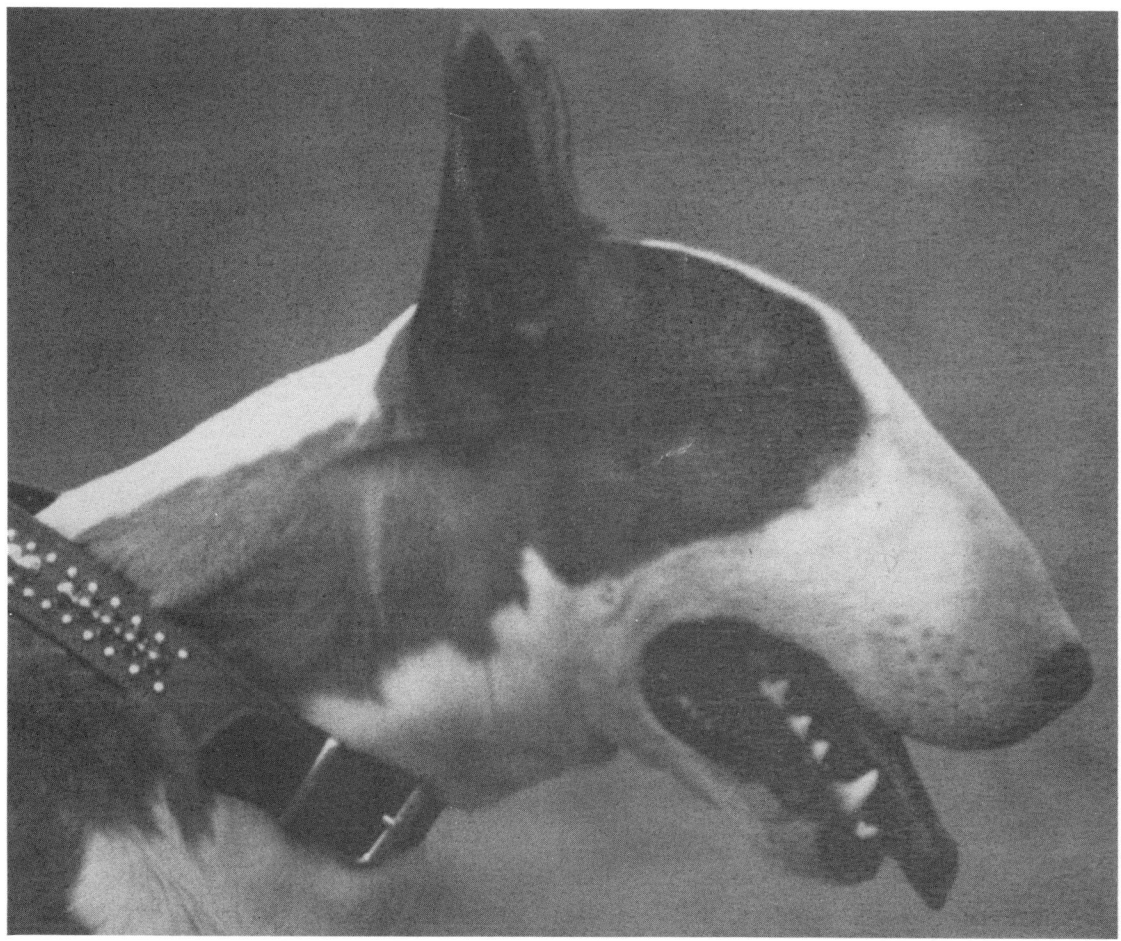

deafness as a result of the loss of color and inbreeding degeneration. Total equality of the white and colored stocks and the free exchange of the breeding lines made the breed much sounder. This is also an example that could be thought provoking with many another breed.

Far too long and far too intensively, the color of the dog was considered of decisive importance, and first-class breeding material was squandered because of slight faults in color. The breeder who deserves this name must recognize that the priorities of dog breeding must clearly lie in a functional anatomical build and in breeding for the desired temperament. Color faults and a complete dentition were overestimated specifically in Germany since the beginning of dog breeding. On the other hand, anatomical faults were accepted too readily.

It is owing to the efforts of Raymond Oppenheimer (Ormandy kennel) that in the numerous, hard-fought differences of opinion among Bull Terrier breeders common sense and tolerance won out in the end. It is certainly the English cynologist who gave the Bull Terrier breed the decisive impulse for more than 40 years with his well-grounded

A Morning Nip, watercolor by Maud Earl, circa 1910 (Dr. Fleig's collection).

II. MODERN FIGHTING DOG BREEDS

This English Bull Terrier was a winner in the Crufts Show, 1994. Thirteen months old. Owned by W. Bimmermann.

knowledge as well as the full use of his commercial connections. It is no exaggeration to say that the Bull Terrier of the twentieth century was very decisively stamped by the ideas of this breeder. The Bull Terrier—and not just this dog breed—owes Raymond Oppenheimer a great deal!

Head fetishism was also a problem with the Bull Terrier. There were bitter fights over the proper head type and over the value of the perfect head. In the 1950s we had Bull Terriers with dream heads, but whose remaining anatomy was deplorably bad. Here, too, common sense triumphed, and the anatomy of the breed has improved enormously in the following twenty years. This was demonstrated in 1972 when Ch. Abraxas Audacity was the first Bull Terrier to win best in show at the famous Crufts dog show. This was a compliment by the rest of the dog world to the Bull Terrier for its first-class anatomy, a proud success for Miss Drummond-Dick, the breeder of the Abraxas Bull Terrier! And in addition to this persistent anatomical improvement, it was also possible to perfect the sought-after dream heads.

The success of the Bull Terrier was by no means limited only to the motherland of England. No, this breed has found admirers in nearly all the countries of the world.

In the show catalog of the Stuttgart Dog Show from the year 1887—the year the Bull Terrier Club was founded in Britain—I found an entry of twenty Bull Terriers, mostly imports, but Bull Terriers already bred in Germany as well! A German breeding center was established around this time in the Braunschweig area with Dr. Wolf, Mr. L. Esche, and Mr. W. Drewes. In 1897 there were two breeding clubs for this breed, one in Braunschweig, the other in Berlin.

The leading personality in Bull Terrier breeding in the German-speaking realm doubtlessly was the Austrian cynologist, Dr. Emil Hauck. The cooperation between Germany and Austria, which began before the turn of the century, was led successfully by him and has now continued for almost a hundred years.

Germany, Austria, Switzerland, the Netherlands, and Belgium are the European countries in which the Bull Terrier has been promoted systematically for many years, whereas they have found less interest so far in the Mediterranean countries.

The Bull Terrier has had wonderful success in the United States, Canada, Australia, and in all the African countries. South Africa boasts a population of about 40,000 Bull Terriers, and here they are also used for hunting on a fairly wide scale. This is certainly the country with the most intensive Bull Terrier breeding.

Before you decide on this highly interesting breed, you must decide if you are willing to train this temperamental and quite independent dog properly. It combines the high

Ch. Polytelis Silver Convention, 1982.

II. MODERN FIGHTING DOG BREEDS

spirits of the wild foal with the stubbornness of the donkey. But if you can train it from a very young age and can make it understand that what you expect of it will be also in its best interests, then it is the best and most cheerful of pupils, brings the best performance to the most difficult dog trial, to tracking or as a search dog in a catastrophe.

Opinions differ concerning its independence. For the ambitious working-dog man, who wants to win dog trials, it is certainly unsuitable, because it lacks the willingness to subordinate itself unconditionally, the tractability of other breeds of working dog. As a rule, it opposes this with extreme stubbornness.

Unfortunately, the Bull Terrier very often attracts the wrong people. It has gotten around that the Bull Terrier can be made vicious, that certain false apostles even preach that we must create a new field of activity in the working-dog arena, to replace the former trial of the rigorous test of the pit.

You do not want a working dog at all, but a proper family companion with all its rights and obligations? Then you have come to the right place. It is a cheerful companion on long walks, but also adapts to the living conditions and opportunities for exercise in the city. It is always a ready playmate for children, but becomes serious if you challenge or threaten it or its people, which it will protect dependably. Through systematic breeding it has acquired a high stimulus threshold, so that it scarcely gets excited over trifles. As a result it is good-natured and does not mistrust strangers. Its self-confidence is reflected in the indifference with which it reacts to all outside influences without aggression. It is important to give it much contact with other dogs during the socialization

What's Wanted of Foyri, 1982.

period, to take action early on if it shows aggression toward others of its kind or other animals. Fighting or cat-killing dogs can be a real nuisance.

Anyone who prizes an independent dog personality, anyone who makes himself the pack leader to this temperamental package of muscle through consistent training will find his ideal dog in the Bull Terrier. We have lived with Bull Terriers for more than twenty years. They overwhelm us with their stormy, ever more demanding love, and in certain situations they have been faithful protectors of family and property. For us the Bull Terrier is the clear number one, our favorite dog, without this making us blind to the faults of the breed.

With pleasure I conclude this chapter with considering the large-framed Ch. Polytelis Silver Convention, which was bred in the Netherlands. It is a male dog

Miniature Bull Terrier. Photo by Isabelle Francais.

that in the opinion of many experts is one of the best and most beautiful ever bred. The imported bitch, What's Wanted of Foyri, is one of the most beautiful colored Bull Terriers. These two animals not only have first-class, breed-typical head, but also exhibit the functional overall anatomy required by the standard. The breed standard requires a maximum of substance in proportion to body size. Unfortunately, this is often misunderstood to mean a requirement for the greatest possible weight. The optimal substance in the Bull Terrier must always be accompanied by long, sturdy leg bones, correct angulation, firm shoulders, and a ground-covering gait. If, in addition, the temperament is typical of the breed, fearless, full of fire, but without aggressiveness, then we have the ideal Bull Terrier.

8. MINIATURE BULL TERRIER

Here again we meet up with our little rat killer, the functions of which we discussed in depth *History of Fighting Dogs*. The Miniature Bull Terrier is the descendent of such famous dogs as Billy and Jack, which once brought wealth and respect to their owners by killing rats in record numbers. These dogs also had a hard time following the banning of fights, but they were always useful, for in the cities of Britain there were countless rats outside the pit as well, so that an effective rat catcher was always in demand.

These Lilliputians had a harder time of it before they made a successful appearance in the show ring. Certainly, the Bull Terrier was always split into two weight classes in shows at the end of the previous century. The large ones competed among themselves, as did the small ones. The limit between large and

Ch. Beewau Enterprise, Miniature Bull Terrier, 1982.

II. MODERN FIGHTING DOG BREEDS

small dogs differed from show to show, and varied between 10 and 16 pounds. In the 1880s, the lightweights were quite popular at the shows. In 1902, however, The Kennel Club had the absurd idea of limiting the maximum weight for the Miniature Bull Terrier to 8 pounds.

The maximum weight was lowered for the small dogs from the misconception that this small, distinctive dog would gain favor as a small "lady's dog." But even in those days the ladies were shocked when their darlings methodically hunted rats and mice. They had actually expected something different from a lapdog.

In other respects this small fighting dog was not necessarily "lady-like" either. An enthusiastic supporter of the Miniature, Lady Evelyn Ewart described her personal experiences as follows: *Now he attacked every cow and was kicked painfully more than once. He also went after every big dog. The only way to divert him from his pugilistic intentions was for his master to leave suddenly during the fight. The fear of being left behind made him abandon his opponent and follow. After being saved many times at the last minute, he met his fate in the jaws of a large, black retriever, which he had attacked in his own kennel.*

An oil painting by the animal painter Euphémie Muraton from around the year 1880 shows us a Miniature Bull Terrier bitch with her puppies. What is striking here is the absolutely perfect, natural prick ear and the first-class head for the time, the excellent bones, and the very typical carriage of the small bitch.

Nonetheless, access to the chambers of beautiful women continued to be denied to this little dog. Lord Decies, an enthusiastic promoter of the small breed, characterizes the appearance of the little fellow when entering a room, it

Ch. Zedbees Zilary, champion bitch, 1982.

asks: *I am here, so where are the rats?* Rats, you were more likely to find in the backyards and stalls, not in the chambers of charming ladies, so a career as the darling of the ladies was out of the question.

There were also nearly unsolvable problems in breeding the Miniatures.

The standard and judges demanded that this dwarf dog should be the true-to-scale copy in all details of its big brother. The large Bull Terrier was bred for a maximum of substance in proportion to its size. How could this be done with the Miniature, with a weight limit of eight pounds? A six-week-old puppy of the Standard Bull Terrier weighs about that much.

The much too low weight limit led to the breeding of flat-ribbed, light-boned dogs. Breeders used breeding stock with clear characteristics of dwarfism, which in turn brought apple-headedness and protruding eyes into the breed. And this with the sought-after Bull Terrier head and small, triangular eyes! Thus, the dwarf became further removed from year to year from the healthy anatomy of its big brother.

A very typical Miniature, the bitch Tiny Mite, from the year 1904, compared to Bloomsburry King, show that it would be difficult to consider Tiny Mite to be a true-to-scale reduction. The weight limit and simultaneous breeding for maximum power and substance are mutually exclusive requirements. Accordingly, in these years the Miniature became a caricature not the image of its big brother.

In the year 1918 The Kennel Club closed its stud book for the Miniature Bull Terrier. There were no further registrations by breeders, and the breed seemed to be extinct.

An early type of Bull Terrier. From an original painting by Chalon in 1830. Photo by Lazi Perenyi.

II. MODERN FIGHTING DOG BREEDS

It continued to live on as a small working terrier, however, even without registration, because the little man was fond of such a small dog. Papers were unnecessary as long as the dog kept the house free of ravenous rats and other vermin. There are reports that in these years there were occasional successful attempts to use the Miniature to hunt foxes and badgers under ground. Above the ground it was effective against all manner of rodents and vermin — and a first-class watchdog in the home!

Colonel Glyn, the well-known Bull Terrier man, founded The Miniature Bull Terrier Club in 1939 and, along with his friends, again gained the recognition of the breed standard from The Kennel Club. A maximum shoulder height of 14 inches was established, and this limit still applies today. Unfortunately, the old mistake of establishing another weight limit, this time at 20 pounds was made again.

How the breed could optimally be made equivalent to the Standard Bull Terrier was shown in 1930 by Hogarth, the Bull Terrier expert. He recommended the systematic use of the smaller dogs from the breeding of the Standard Bull Terriers. Hogarth correctly cited the example of the breeding of Schnauzers in Germany, in which a medium-sized and dwarf breed were bred simultaneously, without this leading to the appearance of apple-headedness, protruding eyes, poor front, and delicate bones in the dwarfs.

The Kennel Club grudgingly

Oil painting by Euphémie Muraton, circa 1880 (Dr. Fleig's collection).

permitted the crossbreeding of the dwarfs remaining in the country and the small with the large. Naturally, these interbreds presented new problems. It was very hard to predict whether there were true dwarfs in the litters or whether the puppies would develop to about the normal size of the Bull Terrier. Several times The Kennel Club placed a time limit of a few years for permission to carry out these crosses. This doubtlessly brought the breed type of the Miniature much closer to the standard of quality of the large dogs. After the time limit ran out, however, and additional crosses were no longer permitted, the quality quickly declined.

I remember very well a conversation with Raymond Oppenheimer on the difficulty of breeding a typical Miniature. We quickly came to agreement that it apparently was not so smart after all to keep the two breeds completely separate in the stud book. Why should the too-large Miniatures not find their place with the Standard Bull Terrier, where the too-small size of the Miniatures could be enormously helpful? If the breed type was supposed to be completely uniform, what was the purpose of separating the breeds? Was it not actually the case in the last century that large and small were actually only separated in different weight classes in the show ring, but not in breeding? I am convinced that such regulation could solve the problems of breeding Miniatures, without affecting in the least the breeding of the Standard Bull Terrier.

In 1970 The Kennel Club permitted incrossing for a period of eight years. The far more important decision, however, was to remove all references to the weight limit from the standard for the breed. This has given the Miniature a great new chance, which, however, breeders have been taking advantage of.

We show the impressive result of this breeding period in Ch. Beewau Enterprise, a Miniature that approaches fairly closely the standard of quality of the Standard Bull Terrier. It is truly an impressive miniaturization of the Bull Terrier. The head and bones would have been unthinkable without the removal of the weight limit and the strong influence from breeding with the larger dogs, as would the substance and well-rounded ribs. The old rat killer has turned into a good, small Bull Terrier.

We must stress the first-class temperament of the Miniature, which is in no way inferior to that of its big brother in this regard. Owing to its small size, it is superbly suited for keeping in the city. It has a fairly strong infusion of terrier blood, which makes it more obedient, but it must be trained not to bark too much.

Unfortunately, I must pour a little cold water on my enthusiasm. The gait and firmness in the shoulder area usually leave much to be desired. This dwarf also frequently stands rather narrowly in the hindquarters. All in all, the quality of its big brother's anatomy has not been achieved so far. There is still much work to be done.

But see for yourself how distinctive a dog a Miniature Bull Terrier can be. With the small size and good quality of the Miniatures, this breed has a real chance to increase its popularity, if it is possible to establish the quality achieved in these foundation first-class dogs in the whole breed. I hope the German breeders soon gain many new members and intensify their cooperation for the good of the breed.

9. STAFFORDSHIRE BULL TERRIER

Around 1860 we left the colored Bull

II. MODERN FIGHTING DOG BREEDS

and Terrier and followed James Hinks and the victory march of his milk-white Bull Terrier through the whole world. It so happens that the color used with the Bull Terrier in the 1920s was taken from the Staffordshire Bull Terrier.

Who are these Staffordshires? In 1860 they were still in their accustomed surroundings, as a dog of the English working class. This was a rough environment, in which the time spent with the dog often was the only ray of light in an environment ruled by the struggle for existence. They had not won riches, the workers in the coal mines, in the steel mills, or in the brick factories in the "Black Country." In the vicinity of Stafford, with its famous china manufacturers, here the old Bull and Terrier was bred particularly intensively. Here they also continued to fight in the pit for their masters. As before, the illegal dog pit continued to be the true test of breeding.

Hardly any portraits of these dogs exist from the nineteenth century, since it would have cost their owners precious money to have had their Staffordshires painted. One of the very few, probably the only clearly dated and signed painting of the early Staffordshire comes from the painter E. Loder from the year 1883. Loder shows a rather uniform breed type in at least four of the five dogs shown. If we compare these animals with the Duke of Hamilton's Bulldogs, we get the impression that the Staffordshire Bull Terrier could actually be the true descendent of the old Bulldog. There is no doubt that the Staffordshire has a substantially higher share of the blood of the old Bulldog than does the Bull Terrier, in which terrier blood predominates.

Head study of a Staffordshire Bull Terrier, circa 1890 (Dr. Fleig's collection).

Yet another highly interesting early document is a head study of the Staffordshire from about the same time. The casual observer might assume that this was an enlarged detail from E. Loder's painting. No, it is a head portrait that was painted on glass by an unknown painter. In the restoration of the picture, it turned out that this oil painting had been painted over an even older painting of a hunting dog. The artist apparently had not had enough money to buy a new piece of glass, so he painted over the old picture. These two paintings complement each other so wonderfully that together they have become a valuable documentation of the history of the breed of the Staffordshire Bull Terrier. One more comment: In these early pictures, the expert is fascinated by the pronounced stop and the ideal ratio of muzzle length to forehead.

In the "Black Country," they of course followed attentively the rapid rise

Tiny Mite, oil painting by F. C. Fairman, 1904.

of the white Bull Terrier as a prized and much admired show dog. It was pointed out bitterly that these dogs were only worthless offshoots of the old breed. For all their beauty, the white dogs had become totally useless for real fighting — degenerate in breeding for beauty! The coveted grapes hung much too high! Here too we can draw very interesting parallels to the present, not about the dogs, but rather about their owners!

Nonetheless, from year to year the outcry increased for the official recognition of the Staffordshire as a separate breed of dog. Joe Dunn set to work with the leading breeders in the country to exchange opinions about how the ideal Staffordshire should look. He spared no effort not to overlook anyone in his inquiries, so as to make use of the experiences of the old-timers. On April 26, 1935, Joe Dunn published in *Dog World* a draft of the breed standard for the Staffordshire. This draft was unanimously adopted at the first meeting of The Staffordshire Bull Terrier Club on May 25, 1935, and was then recognized by The Kennel Club. An old breed was reborn in 1935.

Naturally, there were critics as well. John F. Gordon, one of the energetic promoters of the breed, reported on one of the first shows following recognition by The Kennel Club. A fanatical old-timer placed his hand on his heart and warned all of the spectators: *If a Stafford has nothing here, it is no Stafford. Listen to*

II. MODERN FIGHTING DOG BREEDS

my warning, friends! This is what you intend to do . . . you want a Stafford that no longer has real heart!

Despite these warnings, the new breed went on its way. Old-timers from the "Black Country," in whose families the Staffordshire had made its home for generations, made sure that, despite the shows, great importance was placed on preserving the temperament of the Staffordshire. Joe Mallen, Jack W. Barnard, and H. N. Beilby were trusted by the old breeders, and they proved to be true pioneers of the breed.

As early as 1938 more than 300 puppies were registered. Following a drop-off due to the war, this number shot up to more than 2300 puppies in 1949, then fell back to 1200, and finally reached annual numbers of more than 2000 starting in 1971. In England and the Continent the Staffordshire had clearly surpassed the Bull Terrier in popularity. In 1975 the breed was the third most popular of all terrier breeds, surpassed only by the West Highland and Cairn Terriers. Who would have predicted this success? And these successes achieved only 40 years after recognition!

An important point of the breed standard was and continues to be controversial, and that is the proper size of the breed. At first, in 1935, the size was set at 15 to 18 inches. This was nearly Bull Terrier size. Then it was realized that this produced a dog that was too large and heavy and that it had to be made more mobile and anatomically sound. In 1948 the height

Staffordshire Bull Terrier, oil painting by E. Loder, 1883 (Dr. Fleig's collection).

limit was lowered to 14 to 16 inches in the standard. Breeders were very slow to adopt this change, and many consider it to be wrong even today.

My personal experience is that this upper limit is not taken particularly seriously, and that fairly small deviations on the large side are benevolently tolerated. Concerning the overall anatomy of the breed, I must say that this low-slung dog usually is not a very attractive sight in motion. Here, too, it has been "bred for heads" too long and these points have been overvalued. The stance of the hindquarters is often too narrow, and proper firmness of the shoulders is often lacking. There is still work to be done to achieve a ground-covering gait without a tripping motion.

The judging of the breed cannot and must not be on the basis of its powerful outward appearance. Far more important is its uniquely good temperament. The Staffordshire is also best suited to be fully integrated into the family. The reason it is so extraordinarily popular in Britain is because it causes practically no problems, is not at all nervous, and has a charmingly open temperament.

I must make only a single restriction. It also requires consistent training and shows a good aptitude for it. But, this dog fought its own kind in the pit for a long time, apparently too long a time. And that was not too long ago.

The Staffordshire expert, W. M. Morley, has more than 30 years' experience with the breed. He warns: *In complete contrast to its relations with humans, when the Staffordshire encounters another dog — no matter what its size or outward appearance — the Staffordshire is frequently transformed from a gentleman with excellent manners into a fighting dog machine. Then it is truly liable to do*

Head portrait of *Wardrum Geronimo*, 1981.

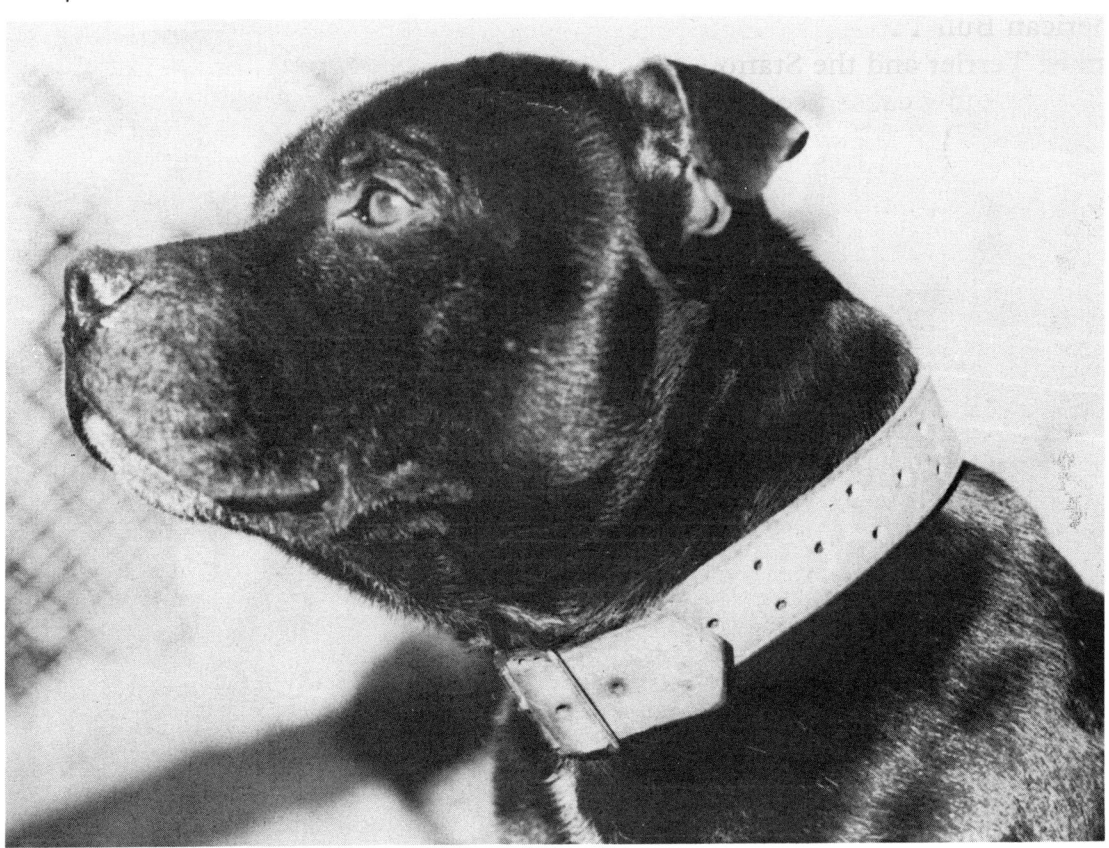

II. MODERN FIGHTING DOG BREEDS

anything. The Staffordshire, however, is not vicious by nature. As a rule, it can be described as pugnacious only if it is given the opportunity to fight. In a certain way it is a mystery to us here.

I do not find the behavior of this dog to be so extremely mysterious, if we consider its past history. I must urgently advise using the socialization phase to train it to tolerate all animals, and dogs, in particular. Particularly in youth, aggression of any kind should not be tolerated. If you follow this advice closely, in the course of training you will become the Staffordshire's pack leader, and you will truly have one of the best and lovable dogs in your house.

10. AMERICAN STAFFORDSHIRE TERRIER

This breed has been recognized internationally under this name since January 1, 1972. The dogs have not had an easy time of it with their name. Formerly they were also called the American Bull Terrier, Pit Bull Terrier, Yankee Terrier and the Stafford Terrier. This repeatedly caused confusion, which should be prevented by the current name.

The ancestor of the American Staffordshire is the familiar Bull and Terrier. This breed came to America with British immigrants around 1860. By leaving Britain, the emigrants also left a country that strictly prohibited dog fights. It is not surprising that in their new home in the United States the old vice soon sprang up again. In the northeastern United States, in particular, dog fights were run professionally starting in 1880. Unfortunately, this perversion of dog keeping still flourishes a hundred years later.

The United Kennel Club was founded in 1898 by C. Bennet in Kalamazoo,

Ch. Hurricane of Judael, 1980.

Michigan. Despite its universal-sounding name, the club had only one purpose: to foster and promote the Pit Bull Terrier, as it was generally called in those days. The club set up its own stud book, but far more important was the issuing of binding competition rules for dog fights, which all UKC members had to obey. In those days there were several periodicals, comparable to the racing forms of horse racing. The magazines reported almost exclusively on fights. These accounts in turn became the basis for future wagering. One of these periodicals was *The Dog Fancier*, another was *Bloodlines*, from which a stream of blood flowed in a figurative sense. But today in the United States, and even in

English Staffordshire Bull Terrier.

II. MODERN FIGHTING DOG BREEDS

Above: Head study of a Staffordshire Bull Terrier, 1830.
Below: English Staffordshire Bull Terrier, International Champion.

Ch. Mari-Don Genie Midnight, American Staffordshire Terrier, 1970.

European countries, publications still appear in which fights are reported on completely openly and advertisements for dog-murdering fighting dogs are carried. One of these American periodicals is the *Sporting Dog Journal*. In a 1977 edition that I came across by accident, puppies from fight-tested parents are openly advertised. There are numerous detailed accounts of fights, and no one seems to be concerned about naming the fight participants and the referees. The $1000 breed still puts food on its master's table. Maybe the $1000 has grown to $10,000 because of inflation, the only change.

The Pit Bull Terrier won great popularity with the help of such prominent supporters as Theodore Roosevelt and John L. Sullivan. During World War I the Pit Bull Terrier symbolized the courage of the American people on large posters. The Pit Bull Terrier together with the English Bulldog documented the brave alliance between the United States and Britain.

Fortunately, not all American breeders succumbed to the intoxication of dog fighting. In the 1920s, the first attempts were made to develop the dog further, to turn the fighting machine into a civilized show dog. Temporal and spiritual parallels to the development in England cannot be overlooked. Interestingly, the standard for the Pit Bull Terrier established in 1921 begins with the following introduction: "In the first place we should not be guided by the outward appearance, our first impression of the dog. Nonetheless, for every dog breed a standard should be established for the outward form to be strived for." The Bull Terrier expert, L. Cabot Briggs, adds to this statement in 1940 the observation that the outward appearance of the Pit Bull Terrier is extraordinarily variable, and that it can be said without hesitation that the appearance of the dog does not play the slightest role. Accordingly, the standard established in 1921 could not have contributed much in the first twenty years to the standardization of the breed type.

Around 1930 American breeders made efforts to obtain recognition of the breed from the American Kennel Club (AKC). This is the only cynological organization in the United States that is recognized in international dog breeding as the umbrella organization for all dog breeds. The top American Staffordshire breeder was Wilfred T. Brandon. On June 10, 1936 the standard of the breed for the American Staffordshire Terrier was officially recognized by the AKC. This opened the stud book and all national and international dog shows to the breed.

In comparison to the Staffordshire Bull Terrier in Britain, it should be noted that its American relative is about 8 centimeters higher at the shoulder and weighs about 5 kilograms more. The

II. MODERN FIGHTING DOG BREEDS

American Bull Terrier breeders had always preferred larger-framed, longer-legged Bull Terriers. These large Bull Terriers were also crossed into the Pit Bulls to a considerable degree and brought more substance and weight to the American dogs.

The Staffordshire Terrier Club of America, which was led for 10 years by Wilfred T. Brandon as president, offered its members the great advantage that it opened the highly interesting American shows to the Staffordshire. The Pit Bulls, on the other hand, were not pedigree dogs and thus could not be registered. Nonetheless, very many fans of the breed still hesitated to join the club, for the new club had a clear policy against all types of dog fighting. Membership and participation and promotion of the dog fights were mutually exclusive positions because big money was still an attraction in dog fighting. But as the dog show offered only prestige to the breeder, the supporters of the American Staffordshire

Head study of *Ch. Patton's Buster Blitz*, 1974.

Ch. Knight Watch Tuckerman, imported to Germany from the United States in the 1970s.

split into two camps. I fear that Mr. Brandon led only a minority on his road to legality.

The Staffordshire Terrier Club of America tried to introduce a new and interesting way to test its members' dogs in the Obedience Trials, which are competitions for working dogs. It soon became evident that the new breed had much to offer for these trials, including intelligence, obedience, and anatomy. As early as 1941, an American Staffordshire was selected "Dog of the Year." Nonetheless, the other side had more to offer to many fans of the breed, not only fame, honor, and work, but large sums of money.

American Staffordshire Terrier.
Photo by Isabelle Francais.

In the 1950s there was an attempt to link up with the remaining pit breeders in the UKC. For several years the AKC recognized the registration of dogs from the pit breeder camp. This had the effect of broadening substantially the breeding basis of the AKC, but this also introduced dogs into the breed that had recently been in the pit, where their "gameness had been freshly tested." After this interim open registration period had run out, however, the separation was complete again, and the two camps still oppose each other whenever possible.

There is an interesting summary of the breeding material of the American Staffordshire Terrier by Richard Pascoe from 1977. He discusses the breed over about 150 pages. Were this not a self-contained book, a kind of short monograph of the breed, the neutral observer of the illustrated material surely would not get the impression that he was being presented with only a single breed of dog. We find long-legged and low-slung, broad and narrow, heavy and elegant types. Anyone who knows something about dog breeds will discover here the types of the Boxer, Bulldog, Bull Terrier, Dogo Argentino, Doberman, and even the Greyhound. This is a collection of ancestors that is far from having been blended into the breed type! From this we must conclude that in 1977 a uniform type corresponding to the breed standard had not yet been achieved.

Colorado v. Simba Camp, German-bred American Staffordshire Bull Terrier, 1980.

Allow me to make a few comments about the standard. Superficially, it requires a "well-put-together dog," that is, one that is anatomically correctly built, stocky but substantial. The dog must always give the impression of great strength and power for its size. According to the standard, cropping the ears is optional. I find this instruction completely incomprehensible, because in practice breeders still crop the ears of their puppies. Do we really believe that the style and elegance of this dog's head requires a cropped ear?

To give the readers my own answer to this question, I wish to consider two dogs. One is an uncropped multiple champion male dog, an original import from the United States, Ch. Knight Watch Tuckerman. The other is a very attractive young male dog of German breeding, Colorado vom Simba Camp. In expression and nobility, I do not think Tuckerman is in any way inferior to the cropped male! The standard leaves it up to the breeders to breed without cropping for a prick ear, drop ear, or half rose ear. Why do the breeders not see the wonderful results of the Bull Terrier breeders after the turn of the century, where they were able in about 20 years to replace the cropped ear with a natural prick ear? After all, the breed does contain the genotype for prick ears!

At an average shoulder height of about 46 centimeters, the American Staffordshire Terrier is a medium-sized, substantial dog, which could be a successful working dog in Germany along the lines of the American model. Its chances as a family dog are surely about the same as those of the Bull Terrier. It too requires consistent training. In this regard we must not overlook that its ancestors were bred purely for dog fighting not that long ago. Its social behavior toward others of its kind is greatly underdeveloped and must be promoted particularly carefully through training. For some years this beautiful dog breed has also found fanciers and been bred in Germany.

Providing your AmStaff with an outlet for his creative energies is a sound idea. This brindle, owned by Eva Lydick of Finwar Kennels, enjoys playing with a tire swing for countless hours.

I see a great danger in that this dog repeatedly attracts the wrong interests. These are the people whose evaluation of the dog is manifested in the stupid question, "Does he bite?" The idea to return the $1000 breed back to its original use, to abuse the dog as a biting machine and for betting purposes, must be fought against with any means possible in the interest of protecting the dog and the honor of man. The breeders of the American Staffordshire Terrier have a great responsibility in placing their puppies, and should also come to clear agreements with the buyers to keep these animals out of the wrong environment.

From an anatomical point of view, the breed in Germany is not yet uniform, and individual types still stand beside one another without a harmonious union. The breed is very young as far as systematic breeding is concerned. The only things that will help here are the strict adherence to the standard, the promotion of breed clubs, and careful planning of possible imports from the United States. The history of the breed has been characterized by exaggeration,

Staffordshire Bull Terrier. Photo by Isabelle Francais.

complete indifference and laxness toward the enforcement of the standard, and the unconditional worship of this "biting machine." There have been very few anatomical faults caused by breeders' excesses. The effort to develop further this beautiful, young dog breed deserves active support.

11. GREAT DANE

We previously presented the Great Dane or Deutsche Dogge in depth in *History of Fighting Dogs* in its development from the old Hunting Dog and the Danish Dog, which represents the first intensive breeding efforts in Germany. How intensively the state of Württemberg, with the old Ulm Dogge, participated in the origin of the systematic breeding of the Great Dane is documented in the show catalog of the *First International Exhibition of Fancy Dogs*, which took place from September 25 to 28, 1887. Under the protectorate of His Majesty, King Carl of Württemberg a total of 663 pedigree dogs were entered in this show, among them the downright unbelievable number of 237(!) Great Danes in various color varieties. Every third pedigree dog at this early dog show was a Great Dane!

There is no doubt that the breed was extraordinarily popular during these years. The big watch and yard dog in Württemberg was the Ulm Dogge, not the German Shepherd. Distributed throughout the region were small breeders, as a rule with one bitch, who met the demand for suitable watchdogs throughout the state. But among them there were also prominent cynologists, including Max Hartenstein from Plauen, already familiar to us from the French Bulldog, who performed pioneer work in the breeding of the Great Dane with his Faust line, and Heinrich Essig from Leonberg, the future father of the Leonberger dog breed. Breeders even visited from Berlin. At the periphery of the show activities, there was much conversation about the future of the breed. From this came the founding meeting of the oldest German breeders' club, Verein für Liebhaber Deutscher Doggen (Association for Fanciers of Great Danes), on January 12, 1888. A short time later this name was changed to the Deutscher Doggen Club (Great Dane Club). It was a highly respected club, because it understood that it must contribute authoritatively to all of the cynological activity in Germany — including the organization of dog shows for all breeds. The club was among the richest of all dog clubs, so that it always received plenty of contributions from its wealthy members.

I would like to document the great reputation enjoyed by the Great Dane at the turn of the century through three quotations. In 1891, Arthur Seyfarth writes: *The fancy and reverence for this aristocratic, grand breed of dog have embraced the widest and most refined circles and extend not only to Germany but to all other dog-loving nations in the whole world. The Great Dane at present has become the most coveted fancy dog in all countries, the dog of the future, the* canis gratissima *in sporting circles, the declared darling of the lady's drawing room, the pride of German cynologists, the German national dog.* Arthur Seyfarth's *Deutsche Colossal-Dogge Lord*, a handsome image of its time, represents the quality that breeders had already reached in 1890. This was possible only because of decades of purebred breeding, though accurate stud bookkeeping was lacking.

Ludwig Beckmann writes in 1894 in his *History and Description of the Breeds of the Dog*: *The Great Dane in its present form is perhaps the most perfect and*

II. MODERN FIGHTING DOG BREEDS

beautiful breed of dog that has ever existed. Beckmann is correct in tracing back the superb anatomy to the hunting tasks of the old Hunting Dog. This was the background for the imposing size, strength, and agility of the dog.

A few years later, Richard Strebel takes up Beckmann's basic ideas almost literally: *A dog that can probably be considered the most perfect in size, symmetry, strength, and elegant movement without exaggeration that has ever been produced in the dog.*

Prince Bismarck, the Iron Chancellor, was accompanied by Great Danes throughout his life. His Tyras the Imperial Dog made world headlines when he misunderstood the hand gestures of the Russian Premier Minister, Prince Gotschakoff, during a lively discussion. Tyras saw in these gestures an attack on his master, charged the noble guest, and pulled him to the ground. Fortunately, the Russian prince was not injured seriously, apologies were accepted, and peace was maintained in Europe. Who could be surprised, however, that the national feelings identified completely with Tyras the Imperial Dog? The breed gained

Champion *Nelly — Walter,* Great Dane, 1912.

many new supporters and admirers.

With the boost from this national movement, the capital of Berlin now became a center of Great Dane breeding along with Württemberg. Around 1890 the breeders in Berlin with their dogs had replaced the Württemberg breeders at the top of German Great Dane breeding. Because of the enthusiasm for the breed, separate breed clubs were founded in many cities and states, which turned out to be quite independent. It was a long and difficult road, which took many decades to travel, before these associations could be united in a single club. But the rival clubs also worked

Great Dane. Photo by Isabelle Francais.

very hard on behalf of the breed. Interesting registration numbers are reported, such as 60 Great Danes in London in June of 1885. At that time these elegant, large dogs were greatly admired in England, although the leading international role of Germany was recognized. Unfortunately, the dog's victory march through England was temporarily slowed to a crawl because of the cropping ban.

What about registrations in Germany? The Frankfurt show in 1888 had 110 Great Danes, the Cologne show in 1889 had 116 Great Danes. Up until the outbreak of World War I, the future of the Great Dane appeared completely unclouded. And then came the hunger, and here again a serious setback.

The very carefully maintained Great Dane stud book reflects the state of the breed in those years. Nonetheless, it is repeatedly protested that a large number of breeders did not make the effort to register the dogs. The registration ages began at six months of age, so that the numbers only give trends but do not give a clear picture of the total number of animals actually bred over the years. Therefore, I will dispense with a more detailed discussion of the numbers, except to say that by 1926 a total of 11,000 Great Danes had been entered in the stud book over 30 years. After the setback during the war, the entries rose sharply in the years of inflation, to about 2150, for example, in 1925. In comparison, in the 1970s about 2000 puppies were registered a year, and about 1800 puppies annually in the 1980s.

A good representative of the breed in 1912, the champion bitch, Nelly — Walter shows a dog breed that still was somewhat shorter in the legs and longer in the back, like Seyfarth's Lord from 1890. The necks of the two animals were somewhat shorter than the modern ideal requires. Both animals, however, are fundamentally sound, large-framed, beautiful dogs, fully consistent with our descriptions by Beckmann and Strebel. They certainly make it understandable why the breed became a kind of German national dog. They were beautiful, good, elegant animals, balanced in their physical functions.

The recognition of the quality of the Great Dane was not limited to Germany or Europe. I find particularly interesting a commentary from England, the motherland of the Mastiff and Bullmastiff. In 1934, we read in the wonderful three-volume *Hutchinson's Dog Encyclopedia*: *The Great Dane today is the most popular dog breed of large dog!* Would you have thought that in the motherland of dog breeding, despite the cropping ban, the Great Dane could actually rank in first place ahead of the native Mastiff? This offers real proof of the high quality of German breeding. It is stressed that the Great Dane is a downright ideal combination of grace and power. It embodies the lightness of the Greyhound and the power of the Mastiff. We should always remember that the reason for the sound anatomy and the mobility of this dog is that it was bred not only for mass and weight, strength of bone and substance but for the preservation of the heritage of the fast and tireless Hunting Dog. In Britain in the 1930s they particularly admired the natural intelligence of the breed. Very few dogs could surpass them. German breeding can certainly also register this as a very important success.

The comparison with Britain makes it abundantly clear that owing to its origin from the large-framed, fast Hunting Dog, the Great Dane stands out favorably from the other molossoid dogs. Interestingly, in Britain it is

II. MODERN FIGHTING DOG BREEDS

repeatedly compared with the Irish Wolfhound or Deerhound. Rawdon Lee lists it in *Modern Dogs* 1894 under Sporting Breeds. We must never overlook this provenance. In the Great Dane, the good anatomy gained in the hunting pack has not been destroyed by the stubborn breeding for mass and weight.

Yet there came a point where human shortsightedness and lust for excess sinned even against this breed. This was the desire for more and more size. It makes absolutely no sense to establish a minimum size for a breed, then a desired mass — significantly higher — and then simply to idealize the shoulder height attained at this mass. This sounds suspiciously like a circular argument.

In 1981, Seyfarth championed shoulder heights of 80 to 90 centimeters, accompanied by body weights of about 60 to 80 kilograms. He coined the concept of the German Colossal Dog. In the early 1890s, the breed standard required at least 76 centimeters, preferably 80 centimeters in males. In 1913 a minimum of 78 centimeters, preferably 82 centimeters, was required. The shoulder heights for the bitches were somewhat lower. Great size is a requirement of the standard. Breeding for color in the Great Dane also drew an inordinate amount of attention in the standard. This again served to divert attention from the real priority of breeding for a good anatomy, because, as far as I am concerned, a good dog cannot have a bad color!

Back to shoulder height. We simply must not overlook that the goal of growth to gigantic size is linked to an abundance of health risks. We find the same thing is true with humans who grow too fast and too long. They usually are not the healthiest!

In the previous century, breeders knew that the Great Dane, in particular, was associated with very specific nutritional problems. The breeding of large, strong-boned dogs was rightly considered to be very difficult. All too often these large dogs were afflicted with rachitis, because many fanciers and breeders simply had neither the knowledge of nor access to the proper foods. We need only consider the massive amounts of nutritional building blocks urgently required by the gigantic dog while it is growing, if it is to attain the strived for size soundly. The Goliath needs the best possible dietary basis and plenty of exercise to reach the maximum shoulder height with a sound anatomy. I have heard rumors, which I take very seriously, that drugs are used to induce growth spurts. This practice is simply dangerous. I have even heard rumors of the use of anabolic steroids!

I have repeatedly warned against exaggerations in all breeds of dog and must do so here as well. In this regard it is simply not logical to say that a dog is more beautiful or valuable simply because it is two or five centimeters taller than its rival. Breeding for extremes usually leads to senseless exaggerations to the detriment of the all-important physical harmony.

Do you recognize the Harlequin dog, Vaun v.d. Nürburg? A truly fine Dane. And if I may add one more thing as a fancier of this dog, not as a Great Dane expert, which I by no means claim to be. Vaun's powerful neck, which, though not quite as arched as we sometimes see, is still admirable. With Vaun we have the impression that all parts of the body stand in a very balanced relationship to one another.

Breeders of Great Danes strive not only for an imposing, anatomically correct form of the dog but also for a dependable temperament. The Great Dane has considerably more temperament, more mobility, as well as a greater impulse to move than we have seen in the other molossoid dogs that we have discussed. These traits are linked in the Great Dane with a moderate to low stimulus threshold, which can lead to unpredictable reactions. Here, too, we repeatedly find reports of shy and nervous dogs, a particularly unattractive sight in this proud dog breed. We must also keep in mind that aggressiveness and shyness are closely related, according to the findings of behavioral researchers.

Because of the size of the dog and a number of unfortunate accidents, we hear warnings that the breed is

Head study of "Fleur Royal," world champion, 1965.

Carlo v. d. Haardburg, male dog, 1979.

II. MODERN FIGHTING DOG BREEDS

Harlequin Great Dane, *Vaun v. d. Nürburg.*

unreliable and that it can be dangerous to humans. This is generally true of all dogs with a low stimulus threshold and an exuberant temperament. Dealing with these dogs is more difficult than with the "good-natured athletes" with bulldog blood.

An expert once told me — it was Philipp Grünig, one of the pioneers of Doberman breeding — that he had spent a lifetime investigating all of the accidents with dogs exaggerated in the sensational press. In 95 percent of the cases, clear incorrect conduct by humans and lack of knowledge of animal behavior had been to blame. In only five percent of the cases had the unpredictability of the individual dog been the triggering factor. This is surely still the case today. But incorrect conduct by humans will always be with us, and ultimately will be just as impossible to eliminate as in the animal. And then, when a Great Dane reacts, a detailed account will appear under headlines in the sensational press, but not with the Pekingese!

Nonetheless, when keeping a Great Dane we must be aware that there is an element of risk, which may be higher with this breed than with many others. There is a reason for a liability law in Germany, according to which the owner of a dog is automatically responsible for the actions of his dog and there is no further investigation of who is to blame. Large dogs are more dangerous, but the dog owner can take steps against this through knowledgeable training and reasonable supervision of his animal. But the breeder, too, can do something here. I am firmly of the opinion that through the systematic breeding for a high stimulus threshold, our dogs should be bred with such strong nerves for daily life that they can deal with the environmental influences calmly and self-confidently. This is infinitely more important than to count to see if a dog has all its teeth in the show ring! This kind of systematic breeding for self-confidence without aggressiveness is no easy task, but it is realizable. This is proved by an impressive number of Great Danes with balanced temperament and strong nerves.

Our modern world is not exactly kind to very large dogs. Large dogs demand much more personal sacrifice from their owners than do medium-sized or small dogs. Anyone who reads Paul Eipper's *Gelbe Dogge Senta (Senta, the Yellow Dog)* will understand, or at least have an idea of, why the Great Dane has so many enthusiastic supporters. The Great Dane Club has about 3000 members. In Switzerland there are 500 members, in the Netherlands 400, to name only two other countries. The breed enjoys undiminished popularity throughout the world, for there are enthusiastic dog fanciers everywhere who admire such large, beautiful dogs.

Even in countries that prohibit cropping, the breed has gained acceptance with medium-heavy ears. How noble the head of the Great Dane can be is shown by the bitch Fleur Royal, a world champion in 1965. The severe, finely chiseled form of this dog's skull is crowned by the form of the cropped ears. Frankly speaking, I am pleased that in many countries of the world the young Great Danes are spared from this procedure. I know what I am talking about, because I also cropped when I was younger, wrapped ears after cropping, and over the years have seen an abundance of badly cropped ears. Would we be better off with a somewhat less aesthetically pleasing effect in the interest of the prevention of cruelty? I admit that this is a heretical comment, which many a fanatical Great Dane

II. MODERN FIGHTING DOG BREEDS

fancier would take offense at! But is there not a grain of truth in this statement?

The Great Dane embodies nobility, size, strength, and elegance as scarcely another breed of dog. This is the first line of the standard for the Great Dane. Could anyone fail to be impressed by the sight of a Great Dane bounding through thd tall grass of a meadow or trotting after a house-drawn coach? And to this is added in this elegant breed a temperament that many perceive as the "soul of the dog."

A companion for the person who takes pleasure in a large, pedigree dog, for the aesthete, who again and again can fall in love with the form and movement of the dog. Anyone who keeps this dog, however, must be aware that he is responsible for keeping this potentially dangerous animal under control. It is a noble breed of dog and truly is the calling card of German dog breeding.

12. BOXER

Here we find the Brabant and the Danzig Bull Biter, smaller now, since bull baiting has slowly been driven out of fashion. To be sure, he has stayed with cattle but now he helps with cattle driving as the butcher's assistant. The leap at the bull's nose is strictly forbidden. Now only the grip on the hind legs is allowed. In this way he keeps restive cattle in check, but he also protects his master's house and yard. He is a medium-sized, sturdy, serviceable dog, who makes himself useful.

A medium-sized, powerful dog, *Athos v. d. Buche.*

In the 1920s a large number of English Bulldogs were brought to the region around Hannover, Germany, and in the following decades more Bulldogs were exported to various German states. The two breeds of dog — Bull Biter and Bulldog — were bred for the same purposes. They often interbred, so that Alfred Brehm, in the first edition of his *Illustrated Animal Life* in 1864, still discusses the Bull Biter and the English Bulldog as separate breeds, but in the second edition of 1886 identifies the Bull Biter and Bulldog as the same breed, and uses in the descriptions for the same dog the name Bulldog in one place and Boxer in another. Apparently the rather English-sounding name tempted him into identifying this German dog in this way. In both editions the character of these dogs is described as extraordinarily aggressive and uncontrollable.

We must assume that the old Bull

Boxer shown at the World Dog Show, 1995.
Photo by Isabelle Francais.

Biter and the English Bulldog were in fact interbred quite intensively in Germany. Ph. Stockmann is certainly correct when he characterizes the separate breeding of the two breeds as follows: *The English, as born geniuses in breeding, understand the supertypical and grotesque and thus produced the modern Bulldog. The practical German, however, did not want to sacrifice the usefulness of his Bull Biter to the monstrous appearance.* A short, precise characterization of the origin of two modern breeds!

Ludwig Beckmann lists the Boxer in the addendum to his great work in 1895 under German Bulldog, and writes that not infrequently in the larger German cities we encounter a large, well-formed, fast, and energetic Bulldog form, which is commonly called the Boxer. *These dogs do not have the deformed appearance of the modern English Bulldog or its undependable character.*

Boxer specialists also agree that the cradle of the German Boxer was Munich. They claim that over the course of decades a broad breeding basis was built up in Munich, the so-called Munich Beer Boxer. Dr. Neumann writes: *Munich was for the Boxer what Ulm or Württemberg was for the Great Dane, a refuge during the decline.* Dr. Neumann thinks that precisely in the Munich region the so abhorred foreign influence of the English Bulldog was largely avoided. In this city the old German Bull Biter blood was for the most part kept pure. This theory is expressly refuted by Richard Strebel. Strebel himself was a passionate Bulldog breeder. He had sold a rather poor Bulldog bitch from his kennel, because she seemed much too light and delicate to him. She was descended from a nearly pure-white Bulldog line. Of all things, she became the ancestor of a new Boxer line. A photograph from 1896 illustrates Strebel's account quite impressively. Strebel emphasizes the extensive similarity between the five white Boxers shown and the English Bulldogs that appeared at that time in German shows. On the other hand, the two dark dogs in the photograph

Boxer breeding in Munich, 1896.

II. MODERN FIGHTING DOG BREEDS

Boxers, *Prinz Mark von Graudenz* and *Kvik*, illustration by R. Strebel, 1904.

embody more of the old Bull Biter breed. Very striking is the small body size of all these Boxer dogs. Note the relation between the body sizes of the men and the dogs.

At one time discussions of the influence of the English Bulldog on the Boxer were always colored by nationalistic emotions —the Boxer, of course, had to be a thoroughly German dog — but today we should be able to view these things more objectively. It would be a slight exaggeration, but certainly not wrong, to say that the English Bulldogs imported to Germany experienced something similar to those brought to France. In both countries the good qualities of the old English Bulldog were used, and native proven dog breeds were crossed with it. In this way the French Bulldog was bred in France, and in Germany — as Beckmann writes — the German Bulldog, which is — as we now know — the German Boxer. Thus, I do not find it at all inappropriate that this German dog has an English-sounding name.

At a dog show in Munich in 1895, there was a trial class for Boxers in which four Boxers were shown. The winner was the male Flocki, which also commands stud book number 1 of the stud book of the Boxer breed. The Boxer Club was founded on January 17, 1896 in Munich, and on March 29, 1896, 50 Boxers were shown at one of the first specialty shows. Their owners were, for the most part, butchers, cattle dealers, students, and small businessmen. As in so many dog clubs, the quarreling began here as well, and the rival German Boxer Club was already founded on January 7, 1897. Many were not happy with the goals established by either club, and even felt harmed by them. The goal was quite clear: move away from the Bulldog type! This did not sit very well, however, with

Head study of English Boxer. Photo by Robert Smith.

English style Boxer. Photo by Robert Smith.

those who owned bulldog-like Boxers, because this breeding goal painfully reduced their economic opportunities, whether in selling puppies or the welcome stud fees. After many years of argument, the clubs came together again. On January 14, 1902 the first breed standard was adopted and the first Boxer stud book was published in 1904. Boxer breeding had begun.

It is interesting that in the standard of the breed in 1902, shoulder heights of 45 to 55 centimeters were required. Thus, Boxers were considerably shorter than today. From 1904 we find two male Boxers that were considered to be quite typical: Kvik and Prinz Mark v. Graudenz, who had a shoulder height of 53.5 centimeters with a chest circumference of 73.5 centimeters.

The Boxer started its victory march through Germany in Munich. World War I brought the familiar difficulties in breeding, but, at the same time, the Boxer withstood its test as a war dog. After the war the Boxer quickly became more and more popular, and on September 22, 1924 the Boxer was officially recognized by authorities as the fifth breed of police dog. This brought new fanciers from the circle of the dog sportsmen.

Thirty years after it was founded, in 1926 the Boxer Club could say proudly: *The old, sleepy Beer Boxer has become a dashing, lively dog, whose attractive features and good size make it particularly suitable as a police and guard dog. The peculiar head and body of the Boxer, which are based on contrasts, are subject to constant transformation, and the strictest breeding selection is required to prevent degeneration either to the Bull Biter or Bulldog side.*

Bazille reports that in 1926 the Boxer Club had 1800 members. At the same time the Great Dane Club had 300 fewer members. Thus, the "little fellow" had already surpassed its big cousin — the Great Dane — in popularity. The Boxer was also larger now. The standard now required a shoulder height of 54 to 60 centimeters, preferably 57 to 58 centimeters in males. Bitches had to be 50 to 58 centimeters at the shoulder. The colors black and white, which had been permitted at the beginning of the history of the breed, were prohibited in 1925 and 1926. This is actually too bad, because the only remaining colors are the typical yellow and red, with and without brindling, with and without mask. Bazille stresses that: *The character of the Boxer is of the greatest importance and requires the most careful attention!* By 1934, 30,000 entries had been made in the Boxer stud book, clear proof of the popularity of the Boxer.

The rest of the story is quickly told. The Boxer is an esteemed dog breed today throughout the world. It is a medium-sized, powerful dog with the character of a true family dog. It has proved itself many times as a working dog. Success with this breed will be achieved only by the dog owner who knows that the Boxer places individual demands on its trainer. It works readily and happily when we know how to challenge it, but as a true offspring of the Bulldog it tends to be independent.

Fundamentally, the Boxer is a decidedly sociable dog, self-confident, with a high stimulus threshold, good-natured, and a wonderful playmate for children. Anyone who takes pleasure in the powerful interplay of muscles of a well-proportioned dog will surely enjoy watching two Boxers at play for hours. It is a beautiful dog.

The Boxer's head shows pronounced independence; it reveals the strength and alert intelligence of this dog. Its undershot bite will not be to everyone's

II. MODERN FIGHTING DOG BREEDS

Head study of the Boxer *Ben v. d. Burg Windeck*.

taste; its Bulldog heritage is openly shown here. Some will also not be particularly fond of the drooling that is not exactly prized in a family dog. Although it is claimed repeatedly that this has been "bred out" through the skill of intelligent breeders, but I ask myself how this can be possible without changing the head form. And, after all, this skull is impressive — highly individual beauty has its price! [EDITOR'S NOTE: Nonetheless, American breeders have successful produced drool-less Boxers for generations—believe it or not!]

In its breeding the Boxer has largely

Mastino Napoletano. Photo by Isabelle Francais.

been spared from fashionable excesses. Size and weight stand in a reasonable relation to each other, so that the dog can move freely and fluidly. Should I deny myself the opportunity to speak out again for the necessity of cropped ears and docked tails? I do so reluctantly, although in other countries I have seen beautiful Boxers that also look quite good with natural ears. Admittedly, they do look better with cropped ears, but . . . I have already said my peace on this subject with the Great Dane and the Bull Terrier.

For people who judge the dog by the stereotype, *Does he bite?*, this probably is not the right dog. For this purpose the Boxer — thank God — is far too good-natured and stable. The high stimulus threshold is comforting and soothing to its owner's nerves. It is an ideal family and companion dog, suited to our times, easy to keep, unproblematic, not a barker, and also absolutely suitable for keeping in the city.

It is not surprising that the Boxer has found an impressive number of fanciers throughout the world and doubtless finds new ones every day.

13. MASTINO NAPOLETANO

The Mastino Napoletano is an ancient dog breed, which was kept pure for centuries by farmers around Mount Vesuvius. It was not rediscovered until 1949 and was recognized as a breed by the FCI. It is assumed that the Mastino is a direct descendent of the ancient Roman fighting dog. The Mastino is a superb watch and guard dog, which through its appearance alone will keep any intruder in check.

With these lines the Molosser Club describes the big favorite of the German Molossus fanciers, which in recent years has developed into the strongest breed of the seven molossoid breeds under the club's care. The "tank of antiquity" — a phenomenal marketing idea of a Mastino fan — has overtaken the old English and French Molossus kept before it in Germany, and today the Mastino is easily at the forefront at shows and in breeding.

In the discussion of the Bordeaux Dog I stated that the whole Mediterranean region from Spain through France to Italy embraced the *old popular sport of dog fighting*. The aggressive hunting dogs first became Bull Biters, then dog fighters. Apparently these Southerners preferred fights between large dogs, unlike England with its Bull and Terrier. All of these southern dog breeds originated from large-framed local boar dogs or herding dogs, crossed with English Mastiffs and Bulldogs.

When we compare the accounts of Roman authors, old illustrations, and statues with the Neapolitan molossoid dogs, we get the impression that these dogs approach nearly optimally the warlike form of the ancient Molossus. The ancient Roman fighting dog has risen from the dead in the Mastino Napoletano.

Nonetheless, with this dog we cannot speak of a *purebred* in the sense of classical dog breeding. This is a breed in which the first halting attempt to work toward a common standard began in 1949. We simply cannot yet expect it to present a uniform breed type. I remember very well that when I was writing my first book, in a well-known kennel I encountered three bitches that differed so much in type that it was hard to believe that all were prize winners at international shows. And this was only about ten years ago. A considerable number of dog generations is required to establish a mature breeding basis. Moreover, heavy dogs of this kind experience far more breeding problems than do other dog breeds.

II. MODERN FIGHTING DOG BREEDS

We should be aware that the first breeders down in Naples came from the lower classes of society. They played by their own rules, with dog breeding as well. Our figure documents that the Mastino did not originate in the villas of the rich, but rather in the huts of the poor. In Naples it was the typical dog of this was its name at that time around Naples — were shown for the first time. These dogs were quite variable in outward form, but Piero Scanziani was fascinated by their particularly impressive size and strength. He could not get their image out of his mind. In the following years, Signore Scanziani

Mastino Napoletano in its Neapolitan homeland.

the butcher, farmer, and night watchman — the big dog of the little man. The ownership of such a dog was a mark of distinction and brought recognition and admiration.

Piero Scanziani is considered the father of the modern Mastino Napoletano. At a show in Castel dell'Ovo in 1946, eight *Cani da presa* — traveled throughout the Naples region and bought more or less purebred puppies for his kennel, Villanova. In 1949 he was finally able to acquire his dream dog, Guaglino. This male became the first champion of the breed. It was entered as the first Mastino in the stud book of the LOI *(Libro delle Origini Italiano)*.

Mastino Napoletano, *Aronne.*

II. MODERN FIGHTING DOG BREEDS

In 1949 the supporters of the breed founded the Societa Italiana del Mastino. Its mission was "the development of the breeding and selection, training and dissemination of the 'Mastino di Napoli.'" In the same year the breed standard was adopted and recognized by the FCI. Guaglino I was the ideal that was written into the standard. This male became the ancestor of the modern breed in the Villanova kennel. Piero Scanziani consolidated the outward and temperamental phenotype of Guaglino through systematic incest and inbred lines.

The leading Italian cynological organization and the new breeders' club came to an agreement, and the Mastino Club was commissioned to start its own stud book. All puppies were first entered here, then examined at 10 to 18 months of age. If they did not meet the requirements, they were deleted from the stud book (LIR, *Libro Italiano Riconosciuti*). If it could be proved that the first three generations of the puppies were registered in the LIR, the official Italian stud book (LOI) was open for registration. All Mastini with recognized national championship titles were also accepted in the LOI.

This all sounds very reasonable on paper, but I must note that there are differences between theory and practice. Even today there are Mastini Napoletano in which no three generations are documented —

Mastino Napoletano, Enrico il Lattatore, at 11 months of age. Owned by Ulrich Brodde; bred by Irmgard Christmann.

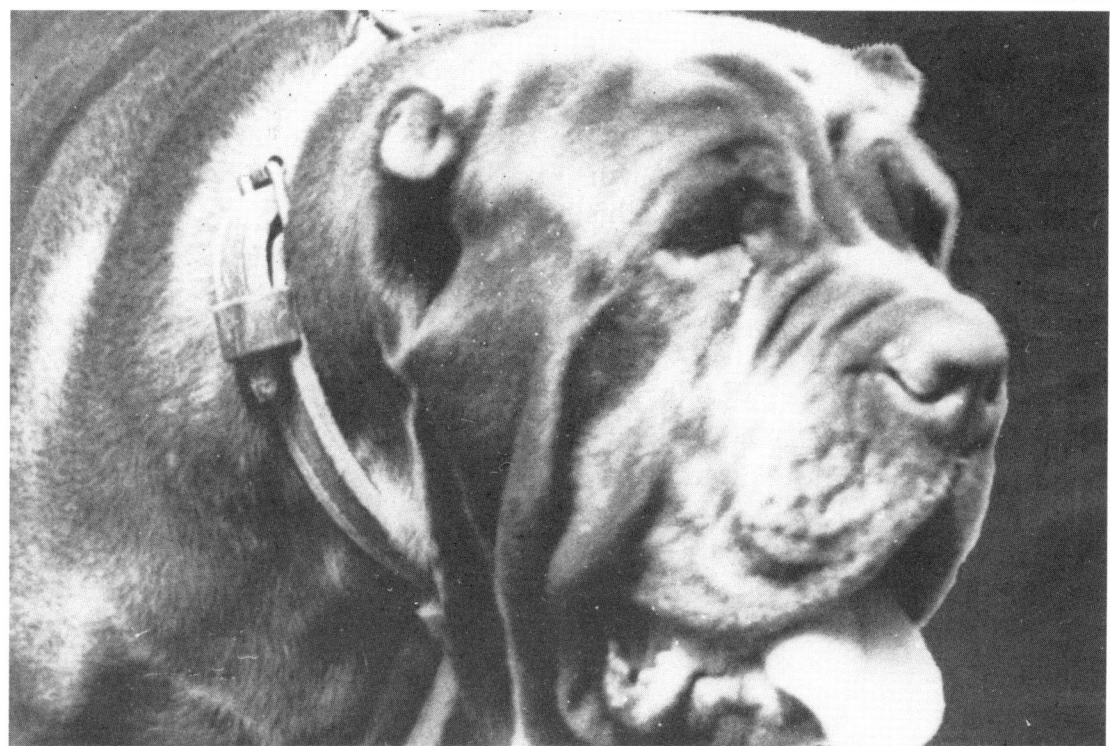

Head study of *Bella Testa diy gilda di Ponzano*.

apparently crossing from unknown sources is still being practiced. It is even more surprising that even the lineage of frequently used champion males is discussed completely openly as being unclear, even though they have pedigrees. It is also said that with many matings it is doubtful whether the indicated father was actually the father of the litter. One breeder made a film to be able to prove that the declared male actually was the sire of the litter. Apparently southern Italy is a suspicious place, and many a cynic would observe that it would hardly be expected to divulge how it breeds its best dogs by recording the correct pedigree — far better to keep this secret and write in different names.

We can therefore state that the breeding of this dog breed is still in its infancy in its homeland.

Nonetheless, the breed has experienced a downright meteoric rise in popularity. From 1950 to 1959 a total of 156 puppies were registered. From 1960 to 1969 the total rose to 905 puppies, and from 1970 to 1979 the number rose

Head study of *Oro*, champion at Naples, 1982.

II. MODERN FIGHTING DOG BREEDS

to a phenomenal 9,737 Mastini Napoletano!

Thus, breeding increased tenfold in the 1970s compared to the previous decade, clear proof of the rapid growth in the popularity of the breed. Was this increase partly responsible for the minimal advances in type achieved in the breed as a whole? With such a boom, was there any selection at all of less desirable dogs? Does such a development — accompanied by very good prices for puppies — do more to hurt or help the breed?

For the cynological observer, the Mastino Napoletano raises the same questions as the English Bulldog. On the one hand, scarcely a dog fancier will not be impressed by the size, strength, and weight of this colossal dog. Many dog fanciers, however, will then — it is to be hoped — understand that the dog is, and must be, a running predator. This leads to the critical question: Can this colossus with a shoulder height of up to 75 centimeters and a live weight of approximately 80 kilograms still be sound?

Let me explain such thoughts with an example. In *Molosser Magazine* in 1982, the male dog Falco della Grotta Azzura is praised as the ideal of the Mastino. The publisher speaks of *a functional structure, sound construction with enormously strong bones and a massive but very noble head.* Then he speaks of an enormous abundance of wrinkles and uniquely well-built shoulders. This is a Mastino *in which the forequarters and hindquarters are well connected by a firm back.*

Unfortunately, I have not seen this dog myself, but Christofer Habig sees in the photographs he published how an

Orfeo di Colosseo Avallu.

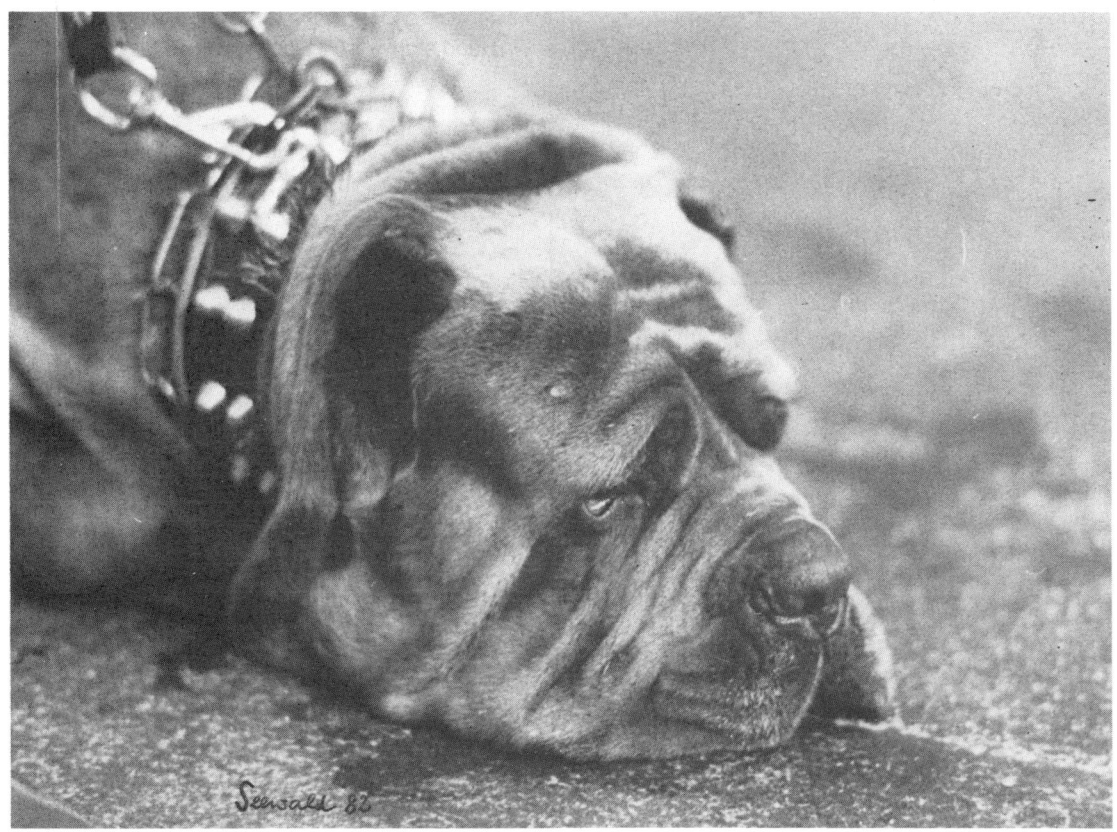

anatomically correctly built Mastino should look. *It simply represents the Mastino to me.*

Unfortunately, my request for permission to use the photographs that, according to Mr. Habig, show the Mastino type so ideally, was refused.

What did I see in the photographs? I saw in these pictures a kind of dinosaur, belonging to the archetype of giant lizards, a dog with a totally disproportional head and neck area, which threw the anatomy of a running predator totally out of balance, making it extremely top heavy. To balance this, the dog was steeply angulated in the hindquarters and was clearly overbuilt. Pronounced tendon weakness in the front, outward-slanting shoulders — a "giant bulldog" with all the anatomical problems we have encountered previously. From the photographs I got the impression that this giant dog could collapse at any moment under its own weight. Falco was supposed to have been about 75 centimeters at the shoulder and have weighed more than 100 kilograms!

Thus, two cynologist can interpret the same pictures so differently! And we are speaking of photographs of one of the most famous "Super Mastini!"

I have discussed the subject of soundness repeatedly in this book and have warned against exaggerations in breeding when they obviously threaten the functionality of a dog breed. I do not grant dog breeders the right to threaten the soundness of the dog breeds entrusted to them through an

Aronne.

II. MODERN FIGHTING DOG BREEDS 173

Mastino puppy, ten weeks old.

excess of mass and weight, or by destroying the natural proportions. Is it not an alarm signal when a specialist of a dog breed seriously emphasizes that in a champion and first-class dog there is in fact still a functional connection between the forequarters and hindquarters of the dog through the back? I would hope this to be true of all dogs!

If I expanded upon this observation it was certainly not with the intention of criticizing a particular dog. This is only a particularly suggestive example of an expert in a breed apparently being prepared to accept serious faults for the sake of a dog's type. For me these are excesses, which, for the dog's sake, should be unacceptable.

Through the friendly help of dedicated Mastino fanciers, I can nevertheless present my readers with very good pictures of the Mastino Napoletano. Particularly impressive is of course the forceful skull of the dog. Who would be surprised that this head alone appears menacing to most people? Let us not forget that war dogs should intimidate through their outward appearance alone, as should watchdogs. This surely also proves that the Mastino was bred chiefly as a large-framed, dangerous-looking watchdog, less so for dog fights. Imagine how vulnerable the abundance of wrinkles makes the dog, what opportunities they would offer its opponent in the dog fight. Compare it with the downright pumped-up head forms of the Bull Terrier and Staffordshire Bull Terrier, where no loose folds of skin offer places to attack.

Very impressive — and beautiful in its way — is the distinctive form of the dog's skull in Oro, winner in Naples, 1982, and then imported to Germany. The experts say: *It shows the ideal type in the head!* There is scarcely another dog breed with such an expressive head!

To give you a little more enjoyment, consider Orfeo die Colosseo Avallu. Have you ever seen more clearly what a dog thinks after a long day at a dog show?

One of the best of the breed was Aronne. As far as experts are concerned, it is the most successful Mastino ever, a dog whose gait gives an excellent impression of the combination of natural strength and flexibility of this giant dog. Unfortunately, Aronne recently went to the eternal hunting ground. His owner, Jürgen Didion, writes: *Aronne was the symbol of the true Mastino both in appearance and character: a true 'tank of antiquity.' His character was fearless and open. He always reacted with the stately calmness of a giant, but at the decisive moment, when he suspected he was in danger, he suddenly became aggressive, without compromise.* This must be it, this combination of physical strength and mobility in the face of danger, that fascinates so many with this breed. In addition to this, the awareness that such a companion can be unconditionally depended on in the face of danger. *This dream of the faithful, four-legged death as the companion haunts the thoughts of many men* (Ulrich Klever).

Murdering dog of the millionaire!

Too vicious! The police confiscated four fighting dogs from a Berlin man!

These are only two of the many headlines that flutter on my desk. I explained previously that the sensational press is not exactly the right medium for discussing cynological questions. It is equally true, however, that we no longer live alone in the wilderness, but rather in the middle of a civilized world — in close contact with our dear neighbors. We also should not take such press campaigns too lightly!

The same press has been misused more than once to run advertisements for the "tank of antiquity." This has had a very unstabilizing effect on prices, to put it mildly. I would suggest to the millionaires with their so valuable possessions that they would be best protected by anything but such a large and powerful dog, especially considering the price of costly antiques!

In *Molosser Magazine* we read the following: *The Mastino has the bad luck of being better suited for marketing than other molossoid dogs.* The publisher speaks of a very unpleasant development with the prices, of the "hanger-on effect" in the selling policies of the breeders, and that the Mastino Napoletano attracts certain kinds of people who are not suited for keeping this dog.

I am in complete agreement with this. I believe that this dog, in fact, belongs only in the hands of the advanced fancier. Many a buyer of a molossoid puppy has absolutely no idea of what it means to have to control physically 60 to 70 kilograms of raging Mastino. Simply letting go of the leash and hoping someone lends a hand surely is not the right approach. These dogs are no playthings for the rich, no status symbols, but complicated living creatures. There are alarm systems and security devices that are far less complicated.

It is hard enough to breed a good Mastino, but the task of finding the right home for the puppies seems much harder to me! To put it rather bluntly,

II. MODERN FIGHTING DOG BREEDS

dogs of this kind attract many idiots, who dream precisely of owning such a dog. The reason why they believe this dog would be exactly the right one for them is more of a question for the psychiatrist than for the cynologist.

Working with such a difficult and interesting breed of dog is a life's work. Breeders face a long, hard road before we find only "Aronnes" in the show ring. The breed would be well served were the marketing of these dogs to soon come to an end. The large sums paid for them harms the breed, and also puts puppies in the hands of owners who ultimately cannot manage this dog and its demands. Increasing sales of adult dogs are the first warning sign! From the bottom of my heart, I hope that every little Mastino will find a good home with understanding people, people who themselves have discipline and are equipped with the inner and outer strength necessary to control such a strong and independent dog.

14. DOGO ARGENTINO

Christopher Columbus discovered the New World in 1492. On his second voyage with 17 ships the Spanish conquerors carried on board their ships, besides weapons, tools, and seed, also

Aronne in Action. Photo by Sigrid Seewald.

war dogs. These trained fighting dogs spread fear and terror among the natives. Within barely 50 years the Europeans had conquered the New World and divided it among themselves.

The country of Argentina was colonized in 1525 by Spain. The new masters were accompanied by their large-framed Mastins. Their first task was to protect the new settlements, and their second was to accompany their masters on the hunt. It turned out that they did excellent service in tracking down escaped slaves, as well as in suppressing the native Indians.

The city of Cordoba was founded in 1573. Here the old fighting dogs were developed further by breeders to perform the tasks in the new country. Soon the onus of dog fighting and bull baiting appeared here as well. Cordoba became the home of a large-framed, white Cordobese Dog (Perro de Pelea Cordobes).

Argentina is a huge country with a diverse geography. In the northwest we find extensive plains, strewn with impenetrable thorny thickets. In the northeast the land is covered with wet tropical forests. A mountain range arises in the south, and in between there is the wide expanse of the Pampas. Colonization brought farmers and ranchers with their immense herds of cattle into the countryside. These herds were preyed on by the jaguar and puma. To make the hunt more interesting, European wild boar were introduced. They soon propagated at an alarming rate and plagued the farmers.

Good dogs were needed to hunt the predators and wild boar. They had to be physically up to the hardships of hunting in this huge country. Although the old Cordobese Dog had the necessary aggressiveness, the willingness to kill,

Hunting in water.

II. MODERN FIGHTING DOG BREEDS

The power and substance of the Dogo Argentino.

and the insensitivity to pain, they lacked the speed, stamina, agility, and scenting ability necessary for the huge hunting areas. On the other hand, the hunting dogs imported from Europe had scenting ability, stamina, and speed to offer, but not the courage and power in the jaws to be able to attack the jaguar, puma, or wild boar. In the meantime, the old, large boar dogs, which were fit for this kind of hard work, had died out in Europe.

Only one dog was suitable for this dangerous hunt: the English Bull Terrier, which had nearly all the desired traits. It lacked only the size and substance for the heavy work.

Dr. Antonio Nores Martinez began in the 1920s with the systematic breeding of a separate — and only — Argentine dog breed. Being a passionate hunter and educated as a geneticist, he set up a breeding program, the goal of which was the ideal hunting dog for predators and wild boar in the specialized Argentine hunting areas. After his fatal hunting accident, his brother, Augustin Nores Martinez, continued his breeding program and led the breed to recognition. Dr. Martinez used as the foundation breeds the old Cordobese Dog and the English Bull Terrier. These breeds form the broad base on which the Dogo Argentino was built. Systematic crosses followed with the Great Dane, whose heritage was power, size, and a very good anatomy. The English Pointer turned the first crossbred with the blunt nose into a working hunting dog with a long muzzle. The Irish Wolfhound was supposed to supply size and speed; the Bulldog, in turn, was to hold onto the seized prey stubbornly. The Bordeaux

On the lookout!

II. MODERN FIGHTING DOG BREEDS

Top: Jump. **Center**: Flight. **Bottom**: Landing.

Dogo Argentino. Photo by Isabelle Francais.

Dog, Spanish Mastin, Pyrenean Mastiff, and Boxer were also used to improve the breed. This dog is a great melting pot of different dog breeds. The Argentines themselves compare it to the history of the origin of the Doberman Pinscher. Together they have produced a white hunting dog with a shoulder height of about 60 to 65 centimeters and a weight of about 35 to 40 kilograms. In this connection the decisive factor for determining which breeds would or would not be used for breeding was success in hunting — hunting over immense areas against dangerous opponents.

Unlike his European colleagues, the Argentine hunter demanded a white dog. Man and dog often hunted the dangerous predator together. The white color protected it from being shot accidentally by the hunter because the predator and hunting dog could easily be distinguished from each other. Argentine hunters also prized a silent hunting dog, which would not waste its energy or alert its opponent prematurely with loud baying.

Concerning the white color, the white coat as such is not an indication of albinism, as long as good pigmentation of the nose, skin, and eye is carefully bred for. We can see the strong influence of the Bull Terriers of that time, however, since it was still bred pure white. Unfortunately, in the first breeding plan, Dr. Martinez concentrated on an extraordinarily substantial male Bull Terrier, which therefore handed down its genes to nearly all subsequent specimens. This male carried the gene for deafness, which is still entrenched in the breed. In the white Bull Terrier the incrossing of the colored Bull Terrier helped, and reduced the problem of deafness down to a maximum incidence of one percent. In the Dogo Argentino, which has been bred only for white over very many dog generations, a considerably higher incidence of deafness must be expected in the puppies. Would the example of the Bull Terrier be worth imitating here as well? A shocking thought for the fan of white dogs, but it could rid the Dogo Argentino of this scourge. And would a colored Dogo really be unattractive? Colored Bull Terriers, despite all resistance, have been a success, to the benefit of the white dogs as well! According to the breed standard, which was recognized in 1949, all colored markings are forbidden except for those in the head region. Even so, will someone eventually dare to break the shackles of the standard?

A dog as beautiful as a dream!

With the Dogo Argentino we are still dealing with a rather young dog breed; moreover, it comes from a country very far from Europe. There are rumors that the breeding conditions in distant Argentina will be at least as difficult to improve as we have discussed previously on our trip to Naples.

In the motherland of Argentina there are supposed to be approximately 3000 Dogos. The centers of breeding, besides Cordoba, are Buenos Aires, La Plate, Mendoza, and San Luis. The Argentine Breeders' Club has about 500 members, and there are rival breed clubs, as well,

II. MODERN FIGHTING DOG BREEDS

which are not recognized by the FCI. The European center of Dogo breeding is Germany, in so far as we can even speak of a center with a total of about 140 dogs in all of Europe. The well-known cynologist, Dr. Erich Schneider-Leyer, imported three Dogos to Germany in 1968. He has invested a lot of effort in this breed. In 1972 the first litter of the breed was produced in Germany. In the next ten years there were only 62 puppies in a total of 13 litters. The few serious promoters of this breed have a hard time of it. Argentina is far away and there are language problems. The breeding stock urgently needs new imports, but first a clear analysis of the stocks must be performed in the motherland so that the imports can be planned accordingly. It costs a great deal of money to do something like this. I hope the breed attracts a patron, who could help to build this breed systematically in Germany as well.

The Dogo Argentino is a very attractive dog. It is an aesthetic pleasure to observe this dog in the countryside. I received expressive photographs from the Netherlands. Just imagine how this white hunter goes hunting in its spacious homeland. Take a look at the motion studies of our figures! See how this dog knifes through the reeds with powerful bounds. Some call to mind the tropical forests of Argentina, and show the passionate hunter on the lookout. I hope that these wonderful photographs will awaken in some of my readers a true interest in this breed of dog.

The hunting ability of the Dogo

A bite like a crocodile!

Argentino is tested regularly in Argentina. On many of the farms of the Dogo breeders there are "test pumas" and "test boars," on which the young dog must prove that it has keenness for hunting. Such testing of course cannot be reconciled with our ideas about preventing cruelty to animals. This also applies, however, to the testing of hunting dogs on the Continent; we could even say overtesting of working dogs for performance sports. I have seen films that show the courage with which half-grown Dogos set on the quite dangerous "test pumas." This was certainly very impressive from the point of view of the interested hunter. Naturally, in Europe there are no jaguars or mountain lions to threaten the herds, and as a rule the wild boar is sensibly hunted with the bullet, so there is little chance of using this dog to hunt in here. Its proper hunting ground is Argentina.

The Dogo Argentino, however, is also used quite successfully by the police and army as a service dog. On the basis of its origin and anatomy, it should be quite successful in working dog competition. In Austria attempts are being made to present the Dogo as a true working dog. And when we examine its list of ancestors, we can see that this dog has many good traits, including the first-class nose.

In the Dogo Argentino we have a rather atypical molossoid dog, but certainly a typical fighting dog. In the tasks for which the Dogo was bred, this breed is a true throwback to the old Hunting Dog.

Experts agree that in Argentina the successful hunting of the jaguar, puma, and wild boar would be impossible without the effective help of the Dogo Argentino. It is a fighting dog that still performs an indispensable service to man in modern times. The immense expanses and the impenetrable landscape demand a hunting companion like this.

To conclude we consider a bitch from Argentina from the early 1970 who captivates with its elegance and superb anatomy. The Great Dane blood is unmistakable. For me this is an uncannily beautiful dog!

In contrast, an original import of the 1980s to Austria, this bitch shows power, substance, and a strong, breed-typical skull.

We are facing a familiar phenomenon that young dog breeds need time before a uniform type can be achieved through many generations of systematic breeding. The breeders and fanciers of this beautiful breed of dog still face a great deal of work.

15. FILA BRASILEIRO

How closely the images resemble each other! In Argentina the Dogo Argentino hunts the jaguar, in Brazil the Fila Brasileiro fights the Onca, the Brazilian panther. From a cynological point of view, the Fila therefore belongs in the first place to the large hunting dogs. It is the hunter of big game but also the protector of the herds. It owes its qualifications for these tasks, however, to its descent from and affiliation with the fighting dogs.

The Fila Brasileiro, too, is descended from molossoid dog breeds, which were brought by the European conquerors to the New World. Argentina was colonized by the Portuguese, who came to the country in the fifteenth century. In Brazil, as well, a center of breeding developed, in which the old breeds were preserved. Here it was the southern part of the state of Minas Gerais.

The original tasks of the Brazilian dogs was to capture escaped slaves,

II. MODERN FIGHTING DOG BREEDS

again a parallel to Argentina. These dogs were so feared that they supposedly captured the escaped slaves and brought them back to their masters without supervision.

In Minas Gerais there were huge farms where the dogs protected the herds from predators, mainly against the dangerous Onca (Jaguar). They were also useful and indispensable for protecting and driving the cattle herds. Even today on the farms the young Fila is tested in the corral to see if it can hold a young steer by the nose or ears long enough for the animal to be captured by men with lassos. This is necessary to brand the feral animals or to administer veterinary treatment. The "farm Fila" does excellent service in driving the herds through trackless country and marshy areas.

The Fila Brasileiro is a fighting dog, hunting dog, cattle driver, and first-class watchdog, all in one!

The old imported breeds were improved further in the late nineteenth and early twentieth centuries through the systematic crossing with European dogs. The Mastiff, Bloodhound, and Bulldog were the decisive crosses for the further development of the breed. Thus, starting in about 1930, we can speak of a breed type of the Fila in the broadest sense. To be sure, there was just as little of a systematic breeding in Brazil as in Naples or Argentina in those years. There was no standard of any kind as a unanimous goal, and the individual farmers bred their own breeds for the tasks they needed them for.

We must single out one man, the attorney Dr. Paulo Santos, for his service in the breeding of the new breed. He discovered his great love for the Fila in 1849, and thereafter created one of the two indigenous Brazilian dog breeds. His breeding goal was a large-framed

Fila Brasileiro, *Clavigo v. d. Hofreite.*

guard and watchdog, very keen and aggressive, and simultaneously a herd-protecting dog and a hunting dog for predators. He visited the large farms of the state of Minas Gerais and found there countless crossbreds of all the large-framed foundation breeds. Corresponding to his selection, he came up with his own ideas about the temperament and anatomy of the new breed. Up to 42 Filas at a time lived in the kennel installation Parnapuan in Santos. From these acquisitions Dr. Cruz created the modern Fila Brasileiro.

On behalf of the Argentine Kennel Club, Dr. Cruz wrote the standard of the breed in 1950. We can assume that the ancestors of all modern Filas once lived in the Parnapuan kennel or on the large farms of Minas Gerais. In order to use the dogs bred on these farms for breeding, a Registro Initial, a register for dogs of unknown pedigree, was established. The farm Filas that were to be entered were evaluated by experts for anatomy and temperament, and if they corresponded to the strived-for type, they were entered in the register. Today this registry — against Dr. Cruz's wishes — is closed. Therefore, the farm Filas can no longer legally be brought into the breeding stock. We must not be misled by such proclamations into thinking that such strict regulation of breeding occurs in Brazil as is the case in Germany, for example.

The first Filas were imported to Germany in 1954. Duke Albrecht von Bayern imported Dr. Cruz's Parnapuan Filas directly. After the Filas overcame certain problems in acclimation, his gamekeeper, Martin Pils, demonstrated that they could also be used to hunt in Germany. The first breeding basis in Germany, however, was not established until 1974. In 1982, 78 German-bred puppies were registered. Therefore, the Fila has also exceeded by far in popularity the large English and French molossoid fighting dog breeds.

The Fila is a difficult dog. Even its breeders and supporters stress that the dog is suitable only for the experienced dog expert. The problem lies in the strength of this stately dog, which has a

Fila Brasileiro, *Boa vom Grünlandhof.*

II. MODERN FIGHTING DOG BREEDS

shoulder height of 70 to 75 centimeters and weighs about 40 to 60 kilograms, combined with a very low stimulus threshold and a strong mistrust of all strangers. Whatever does not belong to the house and yard is attacked. Caution is also advised in dealings with children, because the Fila could misunderstand and become aggressive.

This combination of pronounced natural keenness with a low stimulus threshold makes the dog completely unsuitable for keeping in the city. In the country it needs a large, securely fenced property, plenty of room to move, and a master — or mistress — who controls it. On walks, close attention must be paid to make sure that its pronounced passion for hunting does not break through. Because of its anatomy — and its aggressiveness — it could be a scourge to any wild animal.

In the literature we find a largely unanimous characterization of the dog, whereby keenness and an extraordinary alertness are attributed to it — a dog for an isolated yard, where such an aggressive guard dog can still find a role. The breed standard still requires everything in abundance and the dog must always be very reserved and unfriendly to strangers. On the other hand, shyness and fear are considered to be show-excluding faults. A dog for the would-be animal trainer!

Let me add a word of caution here. With such a temperament, the dog certainly seems ideal for hunting jaguars or for protecting large cattle herds or isolated farms, but not as a house and companion dog. Behavioral researchers have demonstrated conclusively just how closely linked are a low stimulus threshold, aggressiveness, shyness, and fear. Is it possible that the breeders of the Fila have not yet recognized this?

The precise attributes shared by all other breeds of fighting dog, namely natural good-naturedness and calm self-confidence, combined with a high stimulus threshold, are lacking in the Fila. Who can master 60 kilograms of muscle, if it misunderstands any sort of act and attacks in a rage? And how can such a dog be made to stop? Considering all the good anatomical traits of the Fila, it occurred to me that keeping this dog would be like walking around with a loaded pistol in your pocket.

With such a strong and dangerous dog, a standard requirement for distrust of and aggressiveness toward all strangers cannot be justified in the modern world. The Fila is an atypical molossoid dog with respect to character, and can truly be recommended only to very experienced dog experts with very special keeping conditions.

This is all the more regrettable, because the Fila is such an anatomically sound dog, which has by far the lowest rate of hip displasia (HD) of all large molossoid dogs. Only about ten percent of the dogs examined exhibited moderate to severe HD. Consider the striking head type of the breed. Unlike the remaining molossoid dogs with a short muzzle and pronounced forehead, the ratio of muzzle to forehead in the Fila is nearly 1:1. Note the particularly deep muzzle and the very slight stop. Completely unmistakable with this skull is the massive influence of the Bloodhound.

The mobility and power possessed by this dog are shown by the movements of playing dogs. When viewed in this way, the Fila is a typical molossoid dog, a dog with the movements of a fast hunting dog. It is characteristic of it that it prefers to amble when it is moving slowly.

The power and strength of the Fila, as

well as the unmistakable head, is evident even in a sitting dog, such a powerful dog would even be dangerous to the jaguar. Particularly typical of the breed are the pronounced dewlap and the loose skin, which produces wrinkles even in the sitting dog.

The Fila is a large-framed, well-built dog. This dog has been spared the anatomical excesses of other breeds; they would, of course, have been detrimental to the utility of the dog. I know a German-bred male that does not appear overloaded in any way despite all its power. This is a welcome exception compared to the other breeds that we discussed previously.

In recent years a *hard fight to keep the Fila Brasileiro pure* has raged. Dr. Cruz is fighting for the breed he created and is resisting bitterly new crosses with the Mastiff and Mastino Napoletano. He claims that the advocates of such crosses want to turn the old Brazilian working dog into an oversized modern show dog. They would destroy all the work of building up the breed by bringing more foreign blood into the Brazilian national breed. Amazingly, interested parties from Germany have also joined in this dispute, even though the German breeding stock is practically insignificant in comparison to Brazil's. In Brazil 900 Filas were bred in 1975 and 5,000 in 1980. From Germany it is argued that *the history and the type of the Fila, which has grown over decades* is reason to oppose the crossing of the Mastiff and Mastino.

Some people have a rather peculiar idea of history. In two books I have tried to tell the true history of the fighting dog breeds. And history — in the sense of dog breeding as well — extends over

Artus vom Grünlandhof.

Fila Brasileiro. Photo by Isabelle Francais.

a considerably longer period of time than thirty years.

We have seen how Dr. Cruz built up a breed starting in 1950 in a fairly autonomous fashion and how mixed the Fila's ancestry has been, if we follow its history from the original molossoid dogs of the colonial gentlemen. We know from Dr. Cruz himself that the English Mastiff is one of the pillars upon which the Fila was erected. Let us also remember that the old Mastiff was nearly extinct at the end of World War II, and that the old breed was recreated through the imagination and initiative of breeders.

I am opposed to the idea that only the esteemed founder of a dog breed has the right to say what is good or bad for a breed. Every breeder, including the breeder today, has the right, indeed, the duty, to consider whether the breed he loves truly still corresponds in anatomy and character to the requirements of his time. There surely are sufficient cynological reasons to consider a new influx of blood in the Fila.

This breed really should offer animals to dog fanciers that are appropriate for the conditions of the world around us in the next 50 years. But many fanciers would rather stick obstinately to an ideal head type, to desirable color variations, or the like, instead of asking the basic question of whether they are actually breeding a dog for their fellow man and his pleasure.

Since we examine a dog breed not on the basis of its anatomy alone but also on the basis of its character, then I may certainly repeat my question of whether a large-framed, powerful dog in our time should in fact be bred with an extremely low stimulus threshold and have a requirement in the breed standard to consider all strangers as enemies. I see here a true deficiency and nothing but headaches for its owners. Are we breeding our dogs for misanthropic recluses?

Could the crossing of the Mastiff and Mastino be a way to adapt the Fila to the demands of our modern world? Do they not see that there could be reasonable arguments for such a change? I have no intention of getting involved in the dispute in Brazil on either side, and rumor has it the advocates of crossbreeding are even supported by the Brazilian Kennel Club. My comments should serve only to make clear that we should not speak prematurely of a historical heritage and that history alone is not enough of an excuse to forbid contemplation in the present. Genuine historical knowledge of the origin of and the interconnections between the fighting dog breeds should allow us to conduct such discussions impartially.

My hope for the anatomically beautiful Fila Brasliero is that through the efforts of breeders it will be freed of its artificially bred misanthropy. Then surely nothing more would stand in the way of a rapid growth in the popularity of this dog.

16. OTHER BREEDS OF FIGHTING DOG

The idea of the fighting dog being "in" raises the value of the dog for its owner and in public opinion. It is not surprising that many breeders, and many clubs, polish their image by gracing the breed with the effective designation of "fighting dog." Thus, there are cynological dreamers who come up with more than thirty different dog breeds that they classify in this category.

The first fifteen modern breeds that I have presented here are true fighting dog breeds in a cynological sense. The latter two breeds, however, the Dogo

II. MODERN FIGHTING DOG BREEDS

and the Fila, are mixed forms, hunting dog, herding dog, and true fighting dog in one. Here I would like to present two additional dog breeds, which based on their origin are true fighting dog breeds.

A. Tosa Inu

This Japanese dog breed originated in the second half of the nineteenth century. In Japan it is also called Sumo Dog. Sumo fighters are Japanese wrestlers who engage in a very unusual style of wrestling that is already over 1,500 years old. The objective of sumo wrestling is always to stay on your feet despite your opponent's attacks and not to allow your opponent to pin you to the floor or drive you from the ring. Strong and brave young Japanese men enter into a systematic body-building program for years, which turns them into powerful bundles of muscle weighing 100 kilograms or more.

This sumo wrestling is also the basis of the traditional Japanese dog fight. The Tosa Inu is thus a "wrestling dog," and the fights are carried out according to sumo rules. The winner is the dog that presses its opponent to the ground with its body, knocks it off its feet, and holds it to the ground. Biting and growling dogs are disqualified and are banned from further competition.

Tosas who were successful in the sumo fight received a valuable, beautifully decorated cloth apron with the crowning touch of an elaborately braided, thick hemp rope. What was demanded was not the wild fighter, the mauler, but the physically strong dog, courage paired with skill, patience with stamina.

The Tosa Inu originated from the native Shikoku-Inu, an indigenous dog weighing about 25 kilograms and about 55 centimeters high, which closely resembles the European Spitz. These dogs were crossed with European dog breeds, such as the Bulldog, Mastiff, Saint Bernard, and Great Dane. The aim was to breed a larger, more powerful fighting dog. Today Tosas measure 67 to 73 centimeters at the shoulder and weigh 45 to 50 kilograms. The heyday of Tosa breeding was between 1924 and 1933, when it was said that there were more than 5,000 Tosa breeders in Japan.

For Europeans it is hard to comprehend how it is possible to transform a dog breed into a wrestler. This entails going against the dog's natural instincts, against every normal fighting technique of a dog. It seems a likely supposition that dogs that were unsuitable for such fights were used in "normal" dog fights.

There have been few specimens in Europe so far, and only initial attempts at breeding. Despite the history told herein, we have the suspicion that these dogs as a rule also would rather bite than wrestle.

It can hardly be assumed that the importers intend to stage future sumo wrestling matches in Europe. But we do expect very special qualities from these Japanese fighting dogs. Will they fulfill these expectations?

B. Boston Terrier

The homeland of this dog is the state of Massachusetts in the United States. Boston, its capital, gave the dog its name. In the history of the origin of the American Staffordshire Terrier, we know that the English immigrants brought English fighting dog breeds with them to their new home. We have also seen that dog fighting became popular quite quickly. In Boston, Bulldogs and Bull Terriers were crossed. The dogs were bred exclusively for the dog pit, where they were supposed to

Tosa Inu. Photo by Isabelle Francais.

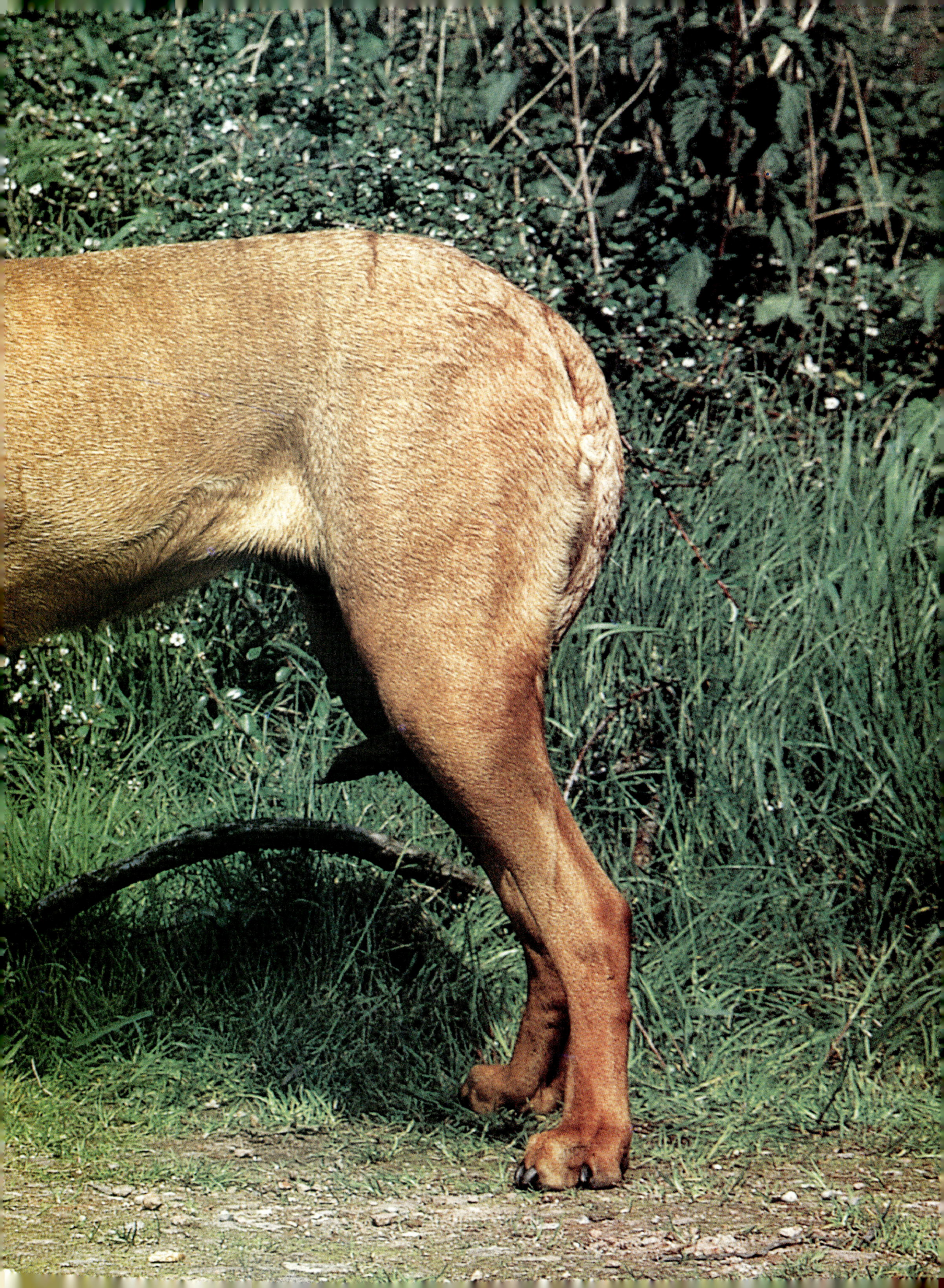

earn their money. These crosses produced dogs of highly variable size and weight. They weighed between 7 and 30 kilograms, which is not at all surprising considering the extreme sizes of the foundation breeds.

Count Bylandt, in his big dog book of 1897, comes to the conclusion that the Boston Terrier and Boxer are one and the same breed. He claims that the club responsible for the Boston Terrier is the Munich Boxer Club (even great cynologists can be mistaken at times). The illustrations show a colorful assortment of German Boxers and American Boston Terriers. He cites for the breed shoulder heights of 35 to 50 centimeters and weights of 7 to 25 kilograms. Despite the assortment of pictures, the illustration of a dog in Boston, Tom, is extraordinarily typical. It could represent just as well the Boston Terrier of the year 1896 and the modern Boston Terrier. An oil painting dating from about 1880 in the United States reveals the quite accurate size relationship between the Boston Terrier and the Bull Terrier at that time. This Bull Terrier portrait in turn documents the influence of the history of the origin of the Dogo Argentino. It should also be mentioned that the Boston Terrier is

Tosa Inu, original imports from Japan.

II. MODERN FIGHTING DOG BREEDS

Playing Tosas.

cropped in the United States, but generally remains uncropped in Europe. Through the subsequent crossing with the French Bulldog, the Boston Terrier in Europe now has the typical bat ear.

It should be noted that the Boston Terrier has been recognized since February 27, 1893 by the American Kennel Club (AKC) as a separate American dog breed. Since then the Boston Terrier has had a loyal following in the United States as the "good little Yankee dog." In England, as well, the dog found committed breeders and fanciers in the 1930s, but remained something of a rarity. We read that in England around 1935 prices of even 2000 pounds for a good specimen of the Boston Terrier were not unusual.

We must understand that over the years, because of changing fashion, the Boston Terrier became more and more

Boston Terrier, *Tom*, 1897.

of a small luxury dog, a lady's dog. The high prices were principally paid for very small dogs. The original fighting dog was turned into a little luxury dog — with all the attendant problems of dwarf breeding.

According to the standard of April 9, 1957, there currently are three weight classes: under 15 pounds, 15 to 20 pounds, and 20 to 25 pounds. The trend is very clearly toward the smallest category, to the small luxury dog. Furthermore, color and uniform markings play a disproportionately large role in the judging. For these reasons, we can probably no longer consider the Boston Terrier to be a fighting dog.

Now I have introduced my readers to a total of seventeen true modern fighting dog breeds. I am certain that many a dog fancier will be disappointed not to find his breed in this listing. I will discuss the premier fighting breed, the American Pit Bull Terrier last, as its existence is largely a matter of nomenclature and American politics.

C. Herding Dogs

There is an impressive number of large-framed breeds of herding dog in many countries in Europe and on other continents. They definitely had molossoid dogs among their ancestors, and the Mastiff, Bulldog, and Bull Biter were also crossed into these breeds. With certain breeds attempts are even made to construct a lineage from the old Tibetan Dog. It is certain that the blood of the ancient Molossus flows in the large herding dog breeds, although it has

Boston Terrier and Bull Terrier, oil painting, United States, circa 1880.

II. MODERN FIGHTING DOG BREEDS

Boston Terrier. Photo by Isabelle Francais.

been thinned to varying degrees through native sheepdog breeds. If the Molosser Club, in fact, wanted to represent all dog breeds with molossoid blood, it would quickly turn into a club that was responsible for the majority of individual breeds.

Cynologically, we should not lump together fighting dogs and large herding dogs. Fighting dogs were bred as war dogs, as hunters of dangerous game, and as participants in animal fights arranged by people.

Herding dogs had, and continue to have, the task of protecting the herds from four-legged and two-legged robbers in all the countries of the world. This, for example, was the task of the German Shepherd Dog, but it does not make them fighting dog breeds. We find large herding dog breeds, which, even today, still defend their herds against predators, among other places in Russia, the former Yugoslavia, Hungary, the Czech Republic and Slovakia, Anatolia (Turkey), northern Italy, Switzerland, Spain, and Portugal.

The main purpose of herding dogs is to herd livestock. Despite having been crossed with large molossoid dogs, "on account of their job" they are of a totally different character than the true fighting dogs presented in this book. The occasional defense against predators is something completely different from the breeding of true boar dogs for hunting or of dogs for animal fighting!

But it is effective advertising to invent fighting dog breeds, because it makes them much easier to exploit commercially. After all, who needs a huge herding dog in our civilized world, what tasks should it take over, where are the herds that it could protect?

One fine example of an imposing herding dog the Mastín Español. It is my fervent wish for all these beautiful herding dogs, that they not be transplanted to an environment in which they no longer have enough living space, where they are degenerated from sound working dogs into wretched kennel dogs. Let us think of the example of the Arctic dogs, which were transplanted from their polar homeland to us. We now have artificial summer training for the sled dogs, and in winter their owners travel hundreds of miles during the months with plenty of snow, in order to provide them with at least somewhat appropriate exercise and training in front of the dog sled. This is very stressful for man and animal! Where in the lowlands of Europe are the big herds, with which the proud herding dogs could find appropriate work? Is taking dog breeds from their original home and locking them in a kennel actually saving them? Cynological ignorance — or pronounced business sense? In the end the dogs will have to pay for it, and human beings will be disappointed!

D. Pug

I am quite sure that many dog fanciers also consider this breed to be a true fighting dog. For a long time the origin of this little "muscleman" was disputed. Many authors believe that it is a descendent of the English Bulldog. Buffon describes it simply as a variety of the Bulldog. Beckmann probably was the first to recognize, in 1895, that the great age of the Pug breed ruled out a descent from the Bulldog. He refers to Holland and its connection to the Far East. Nonetheless, Professor Eugen Seiferle speaks in 1960 of a dwarf dog of unmistakable dogge type, and Ulrich Klever in 1982 sees in it a dwarf dog of unmistakable Molossus type. So, is it a fighting dog after all?

It is true that in nineteenth-century

II. MODERN FIGHTING DOG BREEDS

England, English dwarf Bulldogs were sporadically crossed into the breed. The intention was to "perfect" further the short neck. At the same time the typical Bulldog undershot bite entered the breed. But this is only a very small part of the breed's history.

The specialists of the breed have long agreed that the Pug originated in China, that it is a close relative of the Pekingese and other short-nosed Asian breeds. In particular, detailed skull measurements and comparisons brought the Pug expert, Mrs. Wilhelmine Swainston Godger, to the compelling conclusion that the Pug must be classified with the Asian short-nosed breeds, but absolutely not with the descendants of the Bulldog or Mastiff. Furthermore, the Pug is quite close to its Asian relatives in its entire nature.

Short-nosed dwarf dogs were already bred in China as lady's dogs before the birth of Christ. The Pug reached Holland from the Far East by way of Dutch sailors. Pugs reached England — an event that would be of great significance for Pug breeding — at nearly the same time from Holland and Peking.

Let us now take leave of this charming dog breed, because it does not belong to our circle of the fighting dogs.

E. American Pit Bull Terrier

The emigrants who entered the United States from the "Black Country" of England brought a number of English Bulldogs of old stock, large-framed Bull Terriers, and English Staffordshire Bull Terriers with them to their new home. We have already learned of the high regard good dogs enjoyed in Old England, and it was also expected that these dogs would be able to establish themselves successfully in their new home. Furthermore, precisely in the New World the social hierarchy was based on the ability to assert yourself, on toughness and "gameness." The English also brought the dog fight with them to the New World. Precisely in a population that is fighting for its existence there is the need for diversion in the form of brutal animal fights — *"panem et circenses."* It is documented that in the new homeland of the United

Is this how Pugs fight?

States, as in England, the ownership of a brave dog secured a very high social standing for its owner. I have already presented the historical development of the two breeds, the "American Staffordshire Terrier" and the "American Pit Bull Terrier." In the 1930s, when efforts to gain recognition of the American Staffordshire Terrier by the American Kennel Club (AKC) proved successful, the "Pit Bull Terrier" stayed behind. Thus began the road to the show career for the American Staffordshires. The Pit Bulls, on the other hand, remained closely tied to their original tasks. The United Kennel Club (UKC) assumed responsibility for looking after and supervising the direction of the breed. Then, in the

1930s, the American Dog Breeders Association (ADBA) came into existence. This organization was supposedly founded because the UKC did not throw its weight strongly enough behind the use of the Pit Bulls in the dog fight.

Even today there are still contentious points between the UKC and ADBA. Each club claims that its dogs have more "gameness," that they embody the true type. It must be made clear again here that there is a large number of known ancestors who were registered in both the UKC and the ADBA as "American Pit Bull Terriers." And, interestingly, we suddenly again find these progenitors

Mastin Español, herding dog in Spain.

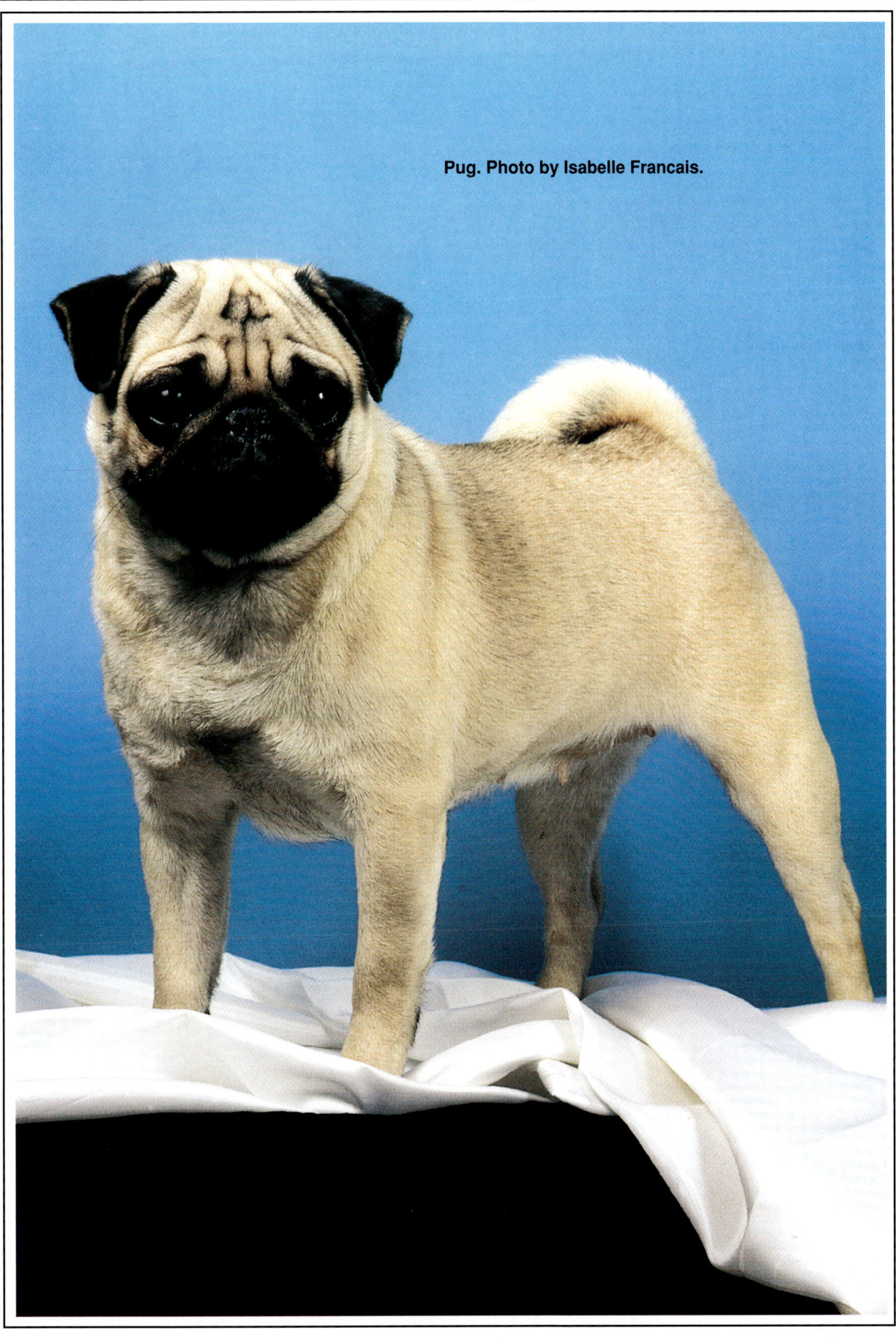
Pug. Photo by Isabelle Francais.

An **American Pit Bull Terrier**, brindle color.

II. MODERN FIGHTING DOG BREEDS

in the line of ancestors of the AKC, but now under the name "American Staffordshire Terrier."

There exists here a considerable number of creeds concerning the "true Pit Bull," and at the same time individual families become prominent, such as the Red Noses and other specific family lines of unique character. If we examine the scene dispassionately, however, we must conclude that when we examine the original English literature on the American Staffordshire or the American Pit Bull Terrier, the illustrated material in fact always reveals a quite uniform and standard type. Moreover, I have also encountered a considerable number of "breed experts," for whom it is objectively impossible to state unambiguously merely by looking at a dog to which breed it actually belongs. This, of course, is not surprising when we consider once more that important progenitors are represented in the lines of ancestors of both breeds.

On its return to Europe, the Pit Bull did not enjoy particularly good fortune. I remember very well how in the early 1970s, with Ed Reid in England, I personally became acquainted with the first American Pit Bull Terriers imported to England. Ed Reid was and is a prominent dog man, but absolutely is not a "softy." He has at his disposal many years of practical experience with all the old English fighting dog breeds. The importation of the American dog had a predominant motive: gameness! In Holland, too, the Pit Bull found its enthusiastic supporters among all those dog fanciers that still clung to the primeval dream of the brave dog. The quite bloody literature from the United States, in which the individual reports of dog fights were reproduced in very clear language, made up part of the bedtime reading of the new supporters. It would also be dishonest for anyone to claim today that the situation is any different in Germany and other European countries. The Pit Bull was preceded by its reputation for being "game," a dog — utterly fearless to the last — that continues to fight to the point of self-sacrifice. Such dogs, of course, attract a certain kind of dog keeper throughout the world.

American Pit Bull Terrier.

If you now wanted to paint a unique picture of this breed from the aforementioned facts alone, however, you would be doing a bitter disservice to the American Pit Bull Terrier! It actually met the same fate as all other fighting dog breeds: On the one hand, it found its fanciers in the lower classes of society. On the other hand, it also continually found fanciers in the solid middle-class society and in the upper class, which wanted

II. MODERN FIGHTING DOG BREEDS

American Pit Bull Terrier Lance's Little Gobbler on top of Cadillac Mountain, Maine. Owner is Lance J. Levy.

precisely such dogs to serve as their life's companions.

This again is best documented on the basis of the United States. A Pit Bull lived in the White House at the side of President Theodore Roosevelt. In 1914 there was a famous big poster on which the chief combatants of World War I were represented by different dog breeds. This poster showed a Dachshund for Germany, a French Bulldog for France, a Borzoi for Russia, and an English Bulldog to represent England. And America — that country was represented by the Pit Bull Terrier, which continued to cling to its old glory.

Pit Bulls, however, were also seen at the side of Franklin Delano Roosevelt in the 1940s in the White House. In the election of 1940, a big rally traveled across the country. Champion Bud, a Pit Bull, took part in the event. Its owner was a famous Golden Glove boxer by the name of Arthur Stubbs. Moreover, Champion Bud was also a "singing dog." It appeared on television and was invited to the White House by Franklin D. Roosevelt. It thus traveled in the best circles!

What I have previously said about the English Staffordshire Bull Terrier, which was greatly appreciated by large segments of the population in the "Black Country," applies in equal measure to large parts of the United States. These dogs enjoy great popularity among a wide variety of citizens in the

Champion Pit Bull Terrier Gideon is a pit dog whose photo hangs proudly in a local restaurant.

II. MODERN FIGHTING DOG BREEDS

Pit Bull Terrier Dolly Danger pouncing through a field.

country. Experts estimate that the population of the Pit Bull is about 20 to 30 times higher than that of the American Staffordshire Terrier! And it simply must be stated here that if it can be demonstrated that a particular breed of dog has such a large number of supporters in a country, then this is rather clear proof that this dog must also have particularly appealing traits for people. And so it does — to the expert the American Pit Bull Terrier is also a very interesting, very beautiful dog, as is proved by the color photographs in this book! Certainly, however, for as long as anyone can remember, it is also true that this dog is kept in the first place for the sake of its character, its temperament, its courage, and less for aesthetic reasons.

This leads me to a very sad story! As much as these dogs have found their supporters in large segments of society, an equally large number of opponents of the breed has appeared throughout the world. Plain and simple, the general public is not prepared to tolerate a dog of such brave character. Accidents have happened — chiefly because the wrong people owned good dogs, who

II. MODERN FIGHTING DOG BREEDS

were not in the position to train them properly and to protect the public from possible danger. It must even be admitted that these dogs were also misused as weapons by their owners! But such misuse is conceivable with practically every breed of dog capable of defending itself; there is no need to develop a separate breed so that criminals can turn them into weapons. As a rule, it would also be possible to do this with any good representative of the breeds generally classified as working dogs.

In the 1980s, in particular, real campaigns were waged in the United States to enact legislation against Pit Bulls and their owners. The well-known American journalist and dog expert, Vicki Hearne, writes on this subject in her book, *According to an estimate by the 'Endangered Breed Association,' 35,000 people brought their dogs, which belonged to the 'bull breeds,' to animal shelters and animal protection organizations, to have them destroyed. The majority of these dogs were Pit Bulls or dogs that somebody took to be Pit Bulls. There were television reports and front pages of newspapers that showed people standing in line with their dogs to have them killed!*

There was an analogous development in England, where the Dangerous Dogs Act was enacted in 1991, which likewise led to a totally incomprehensible and exaggerated campaign against Pit Bulls. Holland also had its own law, which even banned the breeding of these dogs in Holland. According to this law, all these dogs had to be castrated and could only be taken for a walk muzzled and leashed. I can still see the television images from the year 1995, which showed how the dog fanciers in Holland walked on the streets with their Pit Bulls, wearing yellow Stars of David in protest of the banning and condemnation of their dogs.

I simply must take a very strong stand against this development! The public hysteria against these dogs was and continues to be incited by the media in all the affected countries, for the purpose of boosting the ratings or circulation of the tabloid programs and newspapers. At the same time there is no effort to tell the truth. A report that hundreds of thousands of these dogs have integrated themselves peacefully and harmoniously into their environment is of course not news for those with a stake in the media. A single attack, however, even if it occurred in a distant country, generates headlines.

A brave dog breed is unjustly being discriminated against here. It is not the dogs, but the people, who are responsible for the accidents. It must also be emphasized that an American Pit Bull Terrier actually belongs only in the hands of a responsible and sensible dog owner, who is able to give his dog the proper training from the time it is a small puppy.

Responsible dog owners would also do well to work together with the police and the criminal-justice system to act against those Pit Bull owners who misuse their dogs as weapons, who distort the splendid character of this dog. There is a very impressive television program with the title: "MAN IS THE BEAST!" Frankly, there is nothing else to add.

Pit Bull Terrier named Dharma is about to tear apart a heavy garden hose

III. FIGHTING DOGS IN THE FUTURE

Let us not harbor any illusions, the world in which we live is becoming more hostile to dogs every year. German law has long been against the dog. Dogs are property, living creatures that are not differentiated from inanimate objects. The dog owner is liable not only for wrongs committed but, within the scope of the endangerment laws, also for the potential threat his dog poses to others. The only ray of hope is provided by the animal protection laws, but they are very weak ones.

When someone in the city takes his dog on his evening walk, according to most community laws he must always bring a shovel and bucket with him, just in case . . . Have you not also been engaged in pleasant conversation with a dear neighbor, when your Fido had to lift his leg somewhere?

And what is the situation with the longed-for vacation, outside in nature, constantly accompanied by the dog? The joy of the hotel proprietors and the other nice guests is usually so great, that — at vacation time all public and private kennels overflow with dogs.

Kindness to dogs and kindness to children? Both have become very, very rare.

So what are we to do with our fighting dogs? Survivors from a time when the dog truly could still protect its master. A touch of romanticism, sentimentality, nostalgia?

Parallel to the increasingly cold world, sober objectivity, commercialization, growing angst in human beings, there still grows the yearning for a creature that leads the human being back to another, better world. The dog, it is always there for human beings, simply always there, ready to play, to take a walk, to lie quietly beside the master. The dog is always pleased, with each new encounter with its human beings, it gives affection, wants to be stroked. In a hectic world full of anger and discomfort, the dog is there whenever needed. It waits on its human being, until he calls. This must be the explanation for the inner friendship between dog and man. It will also continue to survive in the future, indeed, the yearning for this sort of partnership will only increase.

Now, we must clearly recognize that our fighting dogs are quite demanding dogs. The fighting dog asks more of its owner, but it also gives back this and much more besides. As a rule, a fighting dog is more expensive than other dogs; it costs more to buy, to feed, to care for, and with the large breeds also to house, because it needs a great deal of space to run around in. It requires substantially more in consistent training, in personal care, in responsiveness to its peculiarities. It also offers more — in dog, in personality, in devotion, in willingness to defend. The nature of the fighting dog breed is a treasure, which you must have a feeling for, otherwise you should buy a different dog. I believe — better yet, I am firmly convinced — that these dogs give back to the human being many times more than they receive. This has been my experience over several decades.

Nonetheless, there are certain points to consider concerning the future of our fighting dogs. In the discussion of the individual breeds I repeatedly gave hints about faulty development, misunderstandings, and problems that weigh upon the partnership. I would like to discuss these points once more here.

The fighting dog must fit into the world created by man at the end of the twentieth century, into a world that it could not possibly have been bred for. The most

III. FIGHTING DOGS IN THE FUTURE

Neapolitan Mastiff, *Assunta v. Brabant* with actress Heide Keller.

III. FIGHTING DOGS IN THE FUTURE

important adaptation is the psychological one. A high stimulus threshold and good-naturedness toward man and animal in everyday life are the two basic requirements for dog breeds that must fit into our modern life. Pugnacity and unbridled aggressiveness are completely different from the sensible readiness to defend, which we can expect from a dog that is able to defend itself. Fighting dogs that bare their teeth, are nervous, or tremble not only are distorted images of their breed, they simply do not fit into our time. All the necessary anatomical changes are of secondary importance to the requirement of a reliable temperament.

With respect to the anatomy of our fighting dogs, the breed clubs should carefully and self-critically examine the requirements of the standard to determine which are necessary, sensible, and useful to the breed. Requirements that are detrimental to the breed should be removed. We should no longer stubbornly stick with tradition and pretend that we can breed perfect fighting machines according to physical calculations, even when this turns the dogs into anatomical cripples. And whether the fear-inspiring distorted, and grotesque appearance is still appropriate with certain breeds today also merits consideration. Do not sacrifice the breed type, but get rid of the exaggerations!

From time to time, the daily press has something to say on this subject, but it often does not take time to investigate the topic carefully, if at all. Anyone who examines critically my comments about certain breed characters will surely find a grain of truth in what I say. Moreover, you should not underestimate the tree in your own eye, even when you think you see the famous beam in your neighbor's.

Will you permit me to bring up the subject again of the matter concerning the size and weight of our dogs? Requirements in the standard call for gigantic growth or maximum weight, on the one hand, and the requirement for the optimal soundness of the dog, on the other, are mutually exclusive and are inconsistent with the anatomy of the dog as a running predator. I say, let us get away from the worship of size, away from the foolish requirement for high body weights! We need mobile dogs with strong muscles and tendons. A critical look at the anatomy of the Greyhound would offer interesting opportunities for comparison.

We must not overlook certain medical truths. Rapid growth of the skeleton, heavy bones, and the striving for a maximum of substance frequently cause serious problems in our dogs. The skeleton is held together by muscles and ligaments. If they are overburdened by too much weight, the ligaments become stretched and the muscles become cramped. Such a dog then hangs loosely in the ligaments, and loose ligaments impair the stance and movement of the dog. Putting too much strain on the whole support apparatus leads to pulled muscles, tears, and slow-to-heal lameness.

In the large breeds, growth disorders frequently occur in bones. A particularly dangerous problem is necrosis of the head of the humerus. In this disease the tissue cells of the head of the humerus die, and the cartilage formed in the young dog dissolves instead of getting stronger.

The heavy breeds are also susceptible to fractures, particularly in the area of the elbow joint. We must assume that there is a certain inherited disposition for such fractures, and they usually occur by putting too much strain on the skeleton during play.

Arthritis occurs in the large breeds. Obese dogs, which get little exercise, seem to be particularly susceptible.

A few comments now on movement. In the very young heavy dog, too much can

Head portrait of a Bear Biter, Ag Schleich, circa 1870.

sometimes be more harmful than too little. It is important that the young dog does not waste away, physically and emotionally, in the kennel. It needs sun, light, and space.

Heavy breeds are particularly susceptible to hip displasia (HD). On the basis of mass screenings by the Molosser Club in 1982 of five of the breeds they look after, 16 percent of the Bordeaux Dogs, 27.3 percent of the Bullmastiffs, 30.2 percent of the Mastino Napoletano, 56.6 of the Mastiffs, and 57.8 percent of the Fila Brasileiro have healthy hips. Not an encouraging finding.

I would also like to reiterate the problems of gastric dilation and torsion in the large breeds. There is no patent recipe against bloat. The only useful veterinary advice is too feed frequent, small meals. This too is an indication that we cannot breed too-large and too-massive dogs with impunity, since the weakening of the gastric ligaments practically never occurs in smaller breeds.

I would like to emphasize that I have raised these questions with the full knowledge that things cannot be cleared up in the short term. Animal breeding also means thinking in terms of generations. We are not doing our duty as breeders, if we do not soon include these problems in our plans!

There is a wealth of problems in dog breeding, and this applies to other breeds besides fighting dogs. I viewed it as a responsibility to discuss openly several of them that are the most important to me.

Years ago I had the opportunity to speak at a conference on the origin of the fighting dog breeds. With pictures from my collection I furnished evidence that

III. FIGHTING DOGS IN THE FUTURE

Studies of the French Bulldog, Eugen Kaibalf, circa 1920.

III. FIGHTING DOGS IN THE FUTURE

with many breeds the dogs seemed to be more sound anatomically fifty to a hundred years ago than today. An excess amount of exaggeration actually did not appear in dog breeding until the twentieth century. Breeders in the past constantly had to prove in practice that their dogs could actually deliver the physical or mental performance they strove for. The show ring is not always a sufficient test for this. Sometimes the judges even encourage senseless exaggerations through their decisions.

During the ensuing discussion about recognizable deficiencies in dogs today, caused by wrong requirements of the standard or through erroneous interpretation of the standard, I heard with amazing regularity the comment that this evil can be remedied only in the native land of a breed, because the standard is determined there. As long as such faults are not fought against in the country of origin, they argued, they will be carried to other countries through imports from the country of origin.

This is certainly true, although certainly not unalterable. Can we really expect the international cooperation between all dedicated breeders to fail in the long run because of national egoism? I believe that foreign voices will also be heard in the clubs of the countries of origin, if they truly have something to say. After all, the logic and success of breeding are international.

We have very attractive German fighting dog breeds. The Great Dane and Boxer are first-class calling cards of German dog breeding. Nonetheless, I regret that an old German dog breed is extinct. I am thinking of the old German Bear Biter, such as is shown superbly in, for instance, the prints by Ridinger. Yes, it lives on in the Great Dane and in the Boxer, yet it is a crying shame that the old archetype had to disappear, because it was a very attractive dog of very special character. In *History of Fighting Dogs*, I included a series of good illustrations in the chapter on hunting dangerous game. There are interesting "backbreedings" of old fighting dog breeds, young "old breeds," as we have seen in this book. German breeders have previously brought the extinct Hovawart back to life. Why not the Bear Biter? There certainly still exist in Germany large-framed, shaggy, large dog breeds, and the blood of this dog pulses in the Boxer and Great Dane. A large-framed, shaggy dog, with a good typical temperament, sound and weather resistant — this backbreeding would truly be a real cynological exercise. It would take about twenty years, but such an idea would surely find supporters.

The Italians have their Mastino, the Argentines the Dogo, Brazilians the Fila. None of these breeds was bred seriously until about 30 years ago. And we? I think that imagination and creativity in breeding should not be reserved only for our forefathers. This is required just as much for the backbreeding of an extinct breed as for the improvement of existing breeds today.

For the fancier of the character of a fighting dog, there are interesting breeds to consider, depending on the amount of space available. I wanted to make these more real to the readers of my book. For the large property with a lot of room to run, the Great Dane, Mastiff, and the other large breeds are good choices. The Mastino is another possible choice. But good breeds also get by with less living space, and they can readily be kept in the city as well. These breeds include the Boxer, Bulldog, Bull Terrier, and Staffordshire Bull Terrier.

My book has grown considerably longer than I had planned. It was enjoyable work to extract the essential from a wealth of material, to give the supporters of the fighting dog a complete picture that will

III. FIGHTING DOGS IN THE FUTURE

win new supporters of the dogs.

I remain hopeful that my critical remarks will inspire others to work toward a better future for our dogs. With strength, courage, and vitality, into the future!

With strength, courage, and vitality, into the future!

Hurricane Freya, 1980.

BOOKS FOR FURTHER READING....

H-1075
The Book of the Akita

PS-813
The Boxer

H-1024
The Book of the American Pit Bull Terrier

H-1063
The World of the American Pit Bull Terrier

TS-142
The Truth About the American Pit Bull Terrier

H-1091
The Atlas of Dog Breeds of the World

H-1069
The World of Fighting Dogs

TS-258
Training Your Dog for Sports and Other Activities

BOOKS FOR FURTHER READING....

TS-233 K-9 Body Guards

PS-613 American Pit Bull Terrier

TS-255 Official Book of the Neapolitan Mastiff

TS-141 Pit Bulls Man Stopping Guard Dogs

TS-175 The Most Complete Dog Book Ever Published (A Canine Lexicon)

TS-235 The Working Pit Bull

H-1061 The Complete Dog Buyers' Guide

PS-826 The Great Dane

TS-204 Just Say "Good Dog"

TS-130 Dogs and the Law

INDEX

Page numbers in **boldface** refer to illustrations.

A
A Morning Nip, 118, **120**
Abraxas Audacity, 121
Ag Schleich, **212**
Ajax Of Hellingly, 70, **75**
Alaunt
—of the Butcheries, 35
—Ventreres, 35
Albrecht, Dr., 27
Aldridge Adele, **91**
Aldrovandus, 28
Alexander the Great, 12
Alken, S., 45
American Bull Terrier, 135
American Dog Breeders Association, 200
American Kennel Club, 138, 195, 199
American Pit Bull Terrier, 199
American Staffordshire Terrier, 135, 199
Angehrn, Imelda, 92
Argentina, 176
Aristotle, 12, 19
Arkadian Dog, 28
Aronne, **168**, **172**, **175**
Artus vom Grunlandhof, **188**
Ash, E. C., 44
Assunta v. Brabant, **210**
Assurbanipal, 19
Atlanta Journal, The, 70
Aylva, 18

B
Backbreeding, 214
Ban-dog, 28
Barnard, Jack W., 133
Bazille, F., 106
Bear Biter, 22
Bechstein, J. M., 25
Beckmann, Ludwig, 146, 147, 158, 198
Beewau Enterprise, 130
Beilby, H. N., 133
Bell, 76
Bella Testa diy gilda di Ponzano, **170**
Bellabees Blunder of Bredmardine, **67**
Ben v.d. Burg Windeck, **163**
Bennet, C., 14, 135
Bhotean, **16**
Biggs, Mr., 98
Bismarck (Prince), 147
Bloat, 106
Blome, Richard, 48
Bloodlines, 138
Bloomsbury King, 118, **118**
Boar Dogs, 26
Boar Hound, 22
Boffon, 198
Bordeaux Dog, 101
Boston Terrier, 191
Bouledoguism, 42
Boxer, 26, 155
Boxer Club, 159, 162
Brabant, 23, 155
Brabant Bull Biter, 24
Brandon, Wilfred T., 138, 139
Bredmardine Beelzebub, **78**
Brehm, Alfred, 155
Briggs, L. Cabot, 138
British Dogs, 36

Brooke, Mr., 15
Buffon, 51
Bull and Terrier, 43
Bull Biter, 22
Bull Terrier, 40, 48, 93, 115, 178
Bull Terrier Club, 118
Bull, John, 35
Bulldog, 34, 82, 115
Bulldog Club of England, 42
Bulling Passion, **41**
Bullmastiff, 94
Burkert, Berta, 107
Burton, W., 95
Bylandt, Graf (Count), 90, 102, 108, 194

C
Caillard, 94
Caius, Dr., 28
Canis
—*fam. lagochilus*, 25
—*Molossus Palmatus*, 25
—*porcaritius*, 22
—*pugnax*, 40
—*qui vacaam et taurum prendit*, 22
—*ursoritius*, 22
Carl (King), 146
Carlo v.d. Haardburg, **152**
Castration, 62
Chalon, H. B., 36
Champion Bulling Passion, 42
Chanelle v. Storchennest, **104**
Charpentier, 24
Chien de Nuit, 93, 94
Chimu, **55**
Chincha Bulldog, 10, 25, 55, **55**
Clavigo v.d. Hofreite, **185**
Club Amical, 108
Club for Molosser, 79
Colorado v. Simba Camp, **142**
Cooper, A., 37
Cordobese Dog, 196
Cortelle, M. J., 108
Corvey, 114
Country Life, 66, 70
Crib and Rosa, 37, **38**
Crown Prince, 65
Cruz, Dr., 186
Crystal Palace, 32

D
Dalai Lama, 11, 60
Dalziel, Hugh, **15**, 36, 40, 66
Dangerous Dogs Act, 207
Danish Dogs, The, 48, **52**, **54**, 146
Danzig Bull Biter, 155
Decies (Lord), 127
Denay, 31
Deutsche Colossal-Dogge Lord, 146
Deutsche Dogge, 48
Deutsche Doggen Club, 146
Deutscher Kartell fur Hundewesen, 106
Devonshire, Duke of, 29
Dharma, **208**
Dickin, 76
Didion, Jurgen, 174
Dog, The, 44
Dog Fancier, The, 135
Dog World, 132

INDEX

Dogo Argentino, 175
Dolly Danger, **206**
Double nose, 25, 56
Dougall (Major), 16
Drewes, W., 122
Drummond-Dick, Miss, 121
Drury, 32, 42, 60, 66
D'samu, 17
Dunn, Joe, 132
Dustman, 45, **45**
Dutch Bull Biter, 23

E
Edwards, Syd, **52**
Egan, Pierce, 46
Eipper, Paul, 154
Elephantism, 79
Encyclopedia from the Year 1910, 33
English Bulldog, 82
English Bulldog Club, 37
English Mastiff, 26
English Toy Bulldog, 110
Enrico il Lattatore, **169**
Esche, L., 122
Essig, Heinrich, 146
Ewart, Lady Evelyn, 127

F
Falco della Grotta Azzura, 171, 172
Falsius, Gratius, 26, 27
Farcraft Fidelity, **94**, 99
Farmann, Edgar, 42
Federation Cynologique Internationale, 91
Fehringer, Otto, 90
Fila Brasileiro, 184
Fitzinger, Dr., 25, 53
Flemming, Hans Friedrich von, 23
Fleur Royal, **152**, 154
Flocki, 159
Francke, A. H., 11
French Bordeaux Dog Club, 107
French Bulldog, 57, 107

G
Gastric torsion, 106
Gay, A. and E., 108
Gentleman Farrier, 51
George IV (King), 15
German Bear Biter, 214
German Bordeaux Dog Club, 106
German Boxer Club, 159
German Colossal Dog, 151
Gessner, Conrad, 21
Gideon, **205**
Glyn (Colonel), 129
Gmelin, Professor, 30
Godger, Mrs. Wilhelmine Swainston, 199
Gordon, John F., 132
Goschel, 26
Gotschakoff (Prince), 147
Gotz, Th., 25
Great Dane, 48, 146
Great Dane Club, 154
Great Danish Dog, 51, **51**
Grimmelsburg Bulldog, **112**, 115
Grunig, Phillip, 154
Guaglino, 167

H
Habig, Christofer, 172
Haigh, Norman, 70
Hamilton, Duke of, 37, 91, 131
Harlequin Dane, 52
Hartenstein, Max, 79, 111, 146
Hauck, Emil Dr., 122
Hearne, Vicki, 207

Henry Boynton, 36
Hilzheimer, Professor Max, 25, 56
Hinks, James, 39, 48, 99, 108, 115
Hinks II, James, 115
Hip displasia, 187, 212
History of Fighting Dogs, 8
Hogarth, 129
Hollender (Count), 95
Hollender, Vivian, 94
Hondius, Abraham, 29
Horner, Tom, 66
Hovawart, 214
Hunting Dog, 22, 48, 146
Hurricane Freya, **216**
Hurricane of Judael, **135**
Hutchinson's Dog Encyclopedia, 150

J
Jack in Office, 48, **49**
Jacobsen, Juriain, 48
Jasperdin of Din, **82**, 86
Jennings, L., 43

K
Keller, Heide, **210**
Kennel Club, 71, 99, 100, 118, 127, 128, 130
Klever, Ulrich, 174, 198
Knight Watch Tuckerman, **139**, 143
Kontinental Bulldog-Klub, 90
Ktesias, 12
Kunstler, J., 103, 104
Kuon, Philo, 40
Kvik, **159**, 162

L
Lance's Little Gobbler, **204**
Landseer, Sir Edwin, 48
Lasso vom Antoniushof, 101
Le Chien, 42
Leavitt, David, **84**, 92
Lee, Rawdon, 31, 66, 82, 151
Legh, Peers, 29
Leighton, Robert, 32, 103
Les Chiens D'Arre't, 94
Lewis, G., 48
Libro della Origini Italiano, 169
Libro Italiano Riconosciuti, 169
Lik-Ku, 11
Lindley, 76
Loder, E., 131
Lucy, 37, **38**
Lyme Hall Mastiffs, 29, 66

M
Mallen, Joe, 133
Markusfeld, H. von, 8
Marley, B., 82
Martinez, Dr. Antonio Nores, 178
Masters of the Game, The, 28, 35
Mastiff, 26, 65
—term, 27
Mastin Espanol, 198
Mastino Napoletano, 166
Megnin, Pierre, 18, 42
Menath, W., 44
Minature Bull Terrier, 126
Minature Bull Terrier Club, 129
Modern Dogs, 82, 151
Molosser Club, 101, 106, 166, 212
Molosser Magazine, 74
Molossus, 18
Monk, H. E., 118
Moore, Marie Antoinette, 74
Morley, W. M., 134
Moseley, S. E., 98, 100
Munich Boxer Club, 194

INDEX

Muraton, Euphemie, 127
N
Nebuchadnezar, 12
Necrosis, 211
Nelly —Walter, **147**, 150
Neapolitan Mastiff, 166
Neumann, Dr., 158
Nikias, **18**, 19, 21
Nouc, Hedy, 61
Nydia of Frithend, 71
O
Old English Mastiff Club, 33, 65, 71, 74
Olde English Bulldogge, **84**, 92
Oliff, Douglas B., 74, 76
Oliver, C. R., 70
Oppenheimer, Raymond, 120, 130
Orfeo di Colosseo Avallu, **171**
Orford (Lord), 40
Orgo de l'E'tang des Aieux, **105**
Oro, **170**
Ostmaston Turk, **95**, 98
P
Parnapuan Filas, 186
Pascoe, Richard, 142
Patton's Buster Blitz, **139**
Perro de Pelea Cordobes, 176
Pheraeus, Alexander, 21
Philo-Kuon Standard, 42
Phoebus, Gaston, 101
Pickwick Nicco, **86**, 92
Pickwick Unique, **87**, 92
Pierce, **110**
Pilkinton, Lady Kathleen, 108
Pils, Martin, 186
Pit Bull Terrier, 135, 199
Playing Bulldogs, 43, **43**
Polo, Marco, 13
Polytelis Silver Convention, 126
Preugschat, Werner, 106
Prinz Mark von Graudenz, **159**, 162
Prunella, 70
Pufahl, Maria, 107
Pug, 198
Pugilist, 86
Purst (Viscount), 45, **47**
R
Ratibor, Alexander von (S. D. Prince), 114
Rattle and Clinker, **46**
Reid, Ed, 203
Remus, 70
Riedinger, Johann Elias, 24, 48, 51
Rodney Stone, **79**
Roosevelt, Franklin D., 204
Roosevelt, Theodore, 138, 204
Rosa, 93
S
Sacher, Mrs., 114
Sadler, Justus, 48
Sally of Coldblow, 71
Santos, Dr. Paulo, 185
Scanlan, J. C., 39
Scanziani, Piero, 167
Scheerboom, Mr. and Mrs. L., 70, 76
Schneider-Leyer, Dr. Erich, 183
Seiferle, Professor Eugen, 198
Seyfarth, Arthur, 146, 151
Shikoku-Inu, 191
Siber, M., 13
Sirloin of Pugilist, **83**
Smith, W. R., 31
Snyders, Franz, 48
Societe Canine, 111

Spanish Mastiff, 198
Specht, Friedrich, 53
Sporting Dog Journal, 138
Sporting Magazine, 44, 45
Sportsman's Cabinet, 29, 33
Stafford Terrier, 135
Staffordshire Bull Terrier, 40, 48, 131
Staffordshire Bull Terrier Club, 132
Staffordshire Terrier Club of America, 139
Stephanitz, Rittmeister von, 18
Sting, 46
Stockmann, Ph., 158
Stone, Rodney, 84
Stonehenge, 44, 45
Strabo, 27
Strebel, Richard, 13, 19, 22, 53, 111, 158
Stubbs, Arthur, 204
Studer, 20
Sullivan, John L., 138
Sultane, **102**
Sumo Dog, 191
Swiss Dog Sport, 92
T
Tantzer, Johann, 23
Tauber, Mary Dr., 60
Taurus, 71, 74
Tempesta, Antonie, 48
Terrier-boules, 108
Thorneywood Terror, 95, **95**
Tibetan Dog, 11, **13**, 14
Tibetan Mastiff, **15**, 60
Tiny Mite, 128, **132**
Tom, **195**
Tomtru, **63**
Tosa Inu, 191
Trusty, **44**
Tu-Bo, **61**, 64
Tuite, J. T., 37
Turk, 33, **33**
Turner, Samuel, 13
Turner, Sydney, 33, 82
Tyras, 147
U
Ulm Dogge, 53, 146
United Kennel Club, 135, 200
V
Varro, Marius Terentius, 19
Vaun v.d. Nurburg, 151, **153**
Verein fur Leibhaber Deutscher Doggen, 146
Villatica, 28
W
Wade, William, 66
Walker (Colonel), 66
Walz, B. J., 86
Wardrum Geronimo, **134**
Warwick, 44
Wasp, Child & Billy, 36, **37**
Wegner, Richard N., 56
What's Wanted of Foyri, 126
White, Ben, 37
Wickens, Samuel, 40
Wolf, Dr., 122
World War I, 138
Wosley, **34**
Y
Yankee Terrier, 135
York, Duke of, 28, 35
Youatt, William, 14
Z
Zedbees Zilary, **127**